An Out of Joint and National Theatre co-production

A Laughing Matter
by April De Angelis

A Laughing Matter
First performed at the Yvonne Arnaud Theatre, Guildford
on 17 October 2002

First performed in London at the National Theatre
on 7 December 2002, in repertoire with
She Stoops to Conquer by Oliver Goldsmith

TOUR DATES

12 – 21 Sept 2002 SSTC
Oxford Playhouse
01865 305305 www.oxfordplayhouse.com

26 – 28 Sept SSTC
Lawrence Batley Theatre, Huddersfield
01484 430528 www.lawrencebatleytheatre.co.uk

3 – 5 Oct SSTC
De La Warr Pavilion, Bexhill-on-Sea
01424 787949 www.dlwp.com

17 – 19 Oct ALM
Yvonne Arnaud Theatre, Guildford
01483 440000 www.Yvonne-Arnaud.co.uk

22-26 Oct SSTC & ALM
Salisbury Playhouse
01722 320333 www.salisburyplayhouse.com

29 Oct – 2 Nov SSTC & ALM
Theatre Royal, Bury St Edmunds
01284 769505 www.theatreroyal.org

5 – 9 Nov SSTC & ALM
Everyman Theatre, Cheltenham
01242 572573 www.everymantheatre.org.uk

12 – 23 Nov SSTC & ALM
Birmingham Repertory Theatre
0121 236 4455 www.birmingham-rep.co.uk

30 Nov 2002 – 11 Jan 2003 SSTC & ALM
Lyttelton, National Theatre, London
020 7452 3000 www.nationaltheatre.org.uk

21-25 Jan 2003 SSTC & ALM
Northcott Theatre, Exeter
01392 493493 www.northcott-theatre.co.uk

28 Jan – 1 Feb SSTC & ALM
Cambridge Arts Theatre
01223 503333 www.cambridgeartstheatre.com

6 Feb – 29 Mar SSTC & ALM
Lyttelton, National Theatre, London
020 7452 3000 www.nationaltheatre.org.uk

1 – 5 Apr SSTC & ALM
The Playhouse, Liverpool
0151 709 4776 www.everymanplayhouse.com

8 – 12 Apr SSTC & ALM
Theatre Royal, Bath
01225 448844 www.theatreroyal.org.uk

15 – 19 Apr SSTC & ALM
Theatre Royal, Northampton
01604 632533 www.northamptontheatres.com

Key: SSTC: *She Stoops to Conquer* ALM: *A Laughing Matter*
More information: www.outofjoint.co.uk

out of joint

Founded in 1993, Out of Joint is a national and international touring theatre company dedicated to the production of new writing. Under the direction of Max Stafford-Clark the company has premiered plays from leading writers including Sebastian Barry, Caryl Churchill, Mark Ravenhill and Timberlake Wertenbaker, as well as first-time writers like Simon Bennett.

"One of the finest touring companies in the country" THE TIMES

The Steward of Christendom

Touring all over the UK, Out of Joint frequently performs at and co-produces with key venues including Hampstead Theatre, the Liverpool Everyman & Playhouse, the Royal Court, the Royal National Theatre, Soho Theatre and the Young Vic. By co-producing its work the company is able to maintain a large on-going repertoire as well as premiering at least two new plays a year. Out of Joint is classed as one of the British Council's 'flagship' touring companies, with regular international tours to countries including India, Bulgaria, Russia, Egypt, Brazil, Australia, New Zealand, USA and many parts of Europe. Back home, Out of Joint also pursues an extensive education programme, with workshops in schools, universities and colleges and resource packs designed to accompany each production.

"Max Stafford-Clark's brilliant company" THE SCOTSMAN

The Positive Hour

Out of Joint's challenging and high-profile work has gained the company an international reputation and awards including the prestigious Prudential Award for Theatre. With a permanent commitment from the Arts Council of England, Out of Joint continues to commission, develop and produce new writing of the highest calibre.

"the ground-breaking Out of Joint" THE GUARDIAN

Rita, Sue and Bob Too

out of joint

Director	Max Stafford-Clark
Producer	Graham Cowley
Marketing Manager	Jonathan Bradfield
Admin & Education Manager	Laura Collier
PA to Artistic Director & Assistant Director	Matthew Wilde
Literary Associate	Jenny Worton
Finance Officer	Sharon Smith
Writer in Residence	Mark Ravenhill

BOARD OF DIRECTORS

Kate Ashfield, Linda Bassett, John Blackmore (Chair), Elyse Dodgson, Sonia Friedman, Stephen Jeffreys, Paul Jesson, Karl Sydow

ARE YOU ON THE OJO MAILING LIST?

For information on upcoming shows, tour details and offers, send us your contact details, letting us know whether you'd like to receive information by post or email.

OJO EDUCATION WORK

Out of Joint offers a diverse programme of workshops and discussions for groups coming to see *She Stoops to Conquer and A Laughing Matter*. For more info on our 2002/3 education programme, resource packs, *Our Country's Good* and new writing workshops, contact Max or Laura at Out of Joint.

Post	7 Thane Works, Thane Villas, London N7 7PH
Phone	020 7609 0207
Fax	020 7609 0203
email	ojo@outofjoint.co.uk
Website	www.outofjoint.co.uk

Out of Joint is grateful to the following for their support over the years:
The Arts Council of England, The Foundation for Sport and the Arts, The Baring Foundation, The Paul Hamlyn Foundation, The Olivier Foundation, The Peggy Ramsay Foundation, The John S Cohen Foundation, The David Cohen Charitable Trust, The National Lottery through the Arts Council of England, The Prudential Awards, Stephen Evans, Karl Sydow, Harold Stokes and Friends of Theatre, John Lewis Partnership, Royal Victoria Hall Foundation.

Out of Joint is a registered charity no.1033059

THE ARTS COUNCIL OF ENGLAND

out of joint

PAST PRODUCTIONS & TOURS

2002
Hinterland by Sebastian Barry
- *Hinterland premieres in a National/Abbey, Dublin co-production and Out of Joint is invited to perform A State Affair at the House of Lords.*

2001
Sliding with Suzanne by Judy Upton
Feelgood by Alistair Beaton
- *Rita, Sue / A State Affair is revived for an international tour and Feelgood transfers to the West End, winning the Evening Standard award for Best Comedy.*

2000
Rita, Sue and Bob Too by Andrea Dunbar
& *A State Affair* by Robin Soans
- *Some Explicit Polaroids embarks on two more tours taking in America, France, Lithuania and Germany.*

1999
Some Explicit Polaroids by Mark Ravenhill
Drummers by Simon Bennett
- *Blue Heart has its New York premiere at BAM and Our Country's Good tours further to countries including Brazil, Israel, Bulgaria and Lithuania.*

1998
Our Country's Good by Timberlake Wertenbaker
Our Lady of Sligo by Sebastian Barry
- *Blue Heart is revived for a major international tour while Shopping and Fucking transfers to the West End.*

1997
Blue Heart by Caryl Churchill
The Positive Hour by April De Angelis
- *While Shopping and Fucking begins its first UK tour, Steward of Christendom makes an acclaimed appearance at BAM, New York.*

1996
Shopping and Fucking by Mark Ravenhill
- *Three Sisters and Break of Day is revived for a tour of India and a run at the Lyric, Hammersmith, while The Steward of Christendom and The Queen and I embark on Australian tours in quick succession.*

1995
The Steward of Christendom by Sebastian Barry
Three Sisters by Anton Chekhov
& *Break of Day* by Timberlake Wertenbaker
- *The Queen and I begins a second UK tour while The Man of Mode and The Libertine conclude a national tour with a run at the Royal Court.*

1994
The Man of Mode by George Etherege &
The Libertine by Stephen Jeffreys
The Queen and I by Sue Townsend & *Road* by Jim Cartwright
- *Out of Joint is launched with two double-bills, both of which go on to extensive UK tours.*

Royal National Theatre
South Bank, London SE1 9PX

She Stoops to Conquer and **A Laughing Matter** are co-productions between the National Theatre and Out of Joint. They play in repertory in the Lyttelton Theatre at the National from 30 November 2002.

Within the National on London's South Bank are three separate theatres, the Olivier, the Lyttelton, and the Cottesloe. The chief aims of the National, under the direction of Trevor Nunn, are to present a diverse repertoire, embracing classic, new and neglected plays; to present these plays to the very highest standards; and to give audiences a wide choice.

We offer all kinds of other events and services - short early-evening platform performances; work for children and education work; free live entertainment both inside and outdoors at holiday times; exhibitions; live foyer music; backstage tours; bookshops; plenty of places to eat and drink; and easy car-parking. And the nearby Studio acts as a resource for research and development for actors, writers and directors. We send productions on tour, both in this country and abroad, and do all we can, through ticket-pricing, to make the NT accessible to everyone regardless of income.

The National Theatre was founded in 1963, with Laurence Olivier as Director. For its first years, the Company worked at the Old Vic Theatre, while waiting for the new building on the South Bank of the Thames to be completed. In 1976, under Peter Hall, the move took place. Since its inception, the National has presented nearly 500 plays, and at least five different productions are presented in its three theatres in any one week. Richard Eyre was Director of the Royal National Theatre from 1988 until 1997, when he was succeeded by Trevor Nunn. Nicholas Hytner will become the National's Director in April 2003.

Box Office: 020 7452 3000
www.nationaltheatre.org.uk

Chairman of the Board
Sir Christopher Hogg
Director of the Royal National Theatre
Trevor Nunn
Director Designate
Nicholas Hytner
Executive Director
Nick Starr
Head of Touring
Roger Chapman

Funded by the Arts Council of England
Registered Charity No. 224223

An Out of Joint and National Theatre co-production

She Stoops to Conquer

by Oliver Goldsmith
with a new Prologue and Epilogue by
Stephen Jeffreys

Men:

Sir Charles Marlow	Nigel Cooke
Young Charles Marlow	Christopher Staines
Mr Hardcastle	Ian Redford
Mr George Hastings	Stephen Beresford
Tony Lumpkin	Owen Sharpe
Diggory	Jason Watkins
Landlord / Jeremy	Matthew Sim

Women:

Mrs Hardcastle	Jane Wood
Miss Kate Hardcastle	Monica Dolan
Miss Constance Neville	Fritha Goodey
Pimple	Bella Merlin

Servants and Alehouse Fellows played by
members of the Company

A Laughing Matter

by April De Angelis

cast in alphabetical order:

Edmund Burke / Sam Cautherley / Mr Cross	Stephen Beresford
Charles Macklin / Sir Joshua Reynolds	Nigel Cooke
Peg Woffington / Hannah Moore	Monica Dolan
Mrs Garrick / Mrs Barry	Fritha Goodey
Mrs Cibber	Bella Merlin
Dr Samuel Johnson / Rev. Cumberland / Betty Flint	Ian Redford
Oliver Goldsmith / Theophilus O'Ryan	Owen Sharpe
Cedric Bounce / Mr Larpent	Matthew Sim
James Boswell / Mr Barry / Duke of Kingston	Christopher Staines
David Garrick	Jason Watkins
Lady Kingston / Mrs Butler	Jane Wood

Other parts played by members of the Company

Director	Max Stafford-Clark
Designer	Julian McGowan
Lighting	Johanna Town
Music	Paddy Cunneen
Sound	Neil Alexander
Choreographer	Wendy Allnutt
Assistant Director	Matthew Wilde
Company & Stage Manager	Rich Blacksell
Deputy Stage Manager	Graham Michael
Assistant Stage Manager	Amy Howden
Wardrobe Managers	James Button
	Nina Kendall
Production Manager	Phil Cameron for Background
Costume Supervisor	Hattie Barsby
Casting	Maggie Lunn and Gabrielle Dawes
Company Voice Work	Patsy Rodenburg
Dialect Coach	William Conacher
Production Electrician	Lars Kincaid
Design Assistant	Vicki Cowan
Production Photography	John Haynes
Rehearsal Photography	Graham Michael
Print Design	Iain Lanyon

For Out of Joint:

Producer	Graham Cowley
Marketing Manager (to Sept '02)	Alice Lascelles
(from Sept '02)	Jonathan Bradfield
Administration & Education Manager	Laura Collier

Production credits:

Set built by Scenery Jessell
Props, costumes and wigs partly supplied by the National
Theatre. Additional props and furniture supplied by Souvenir
Show transport by Southern Van Lines
Lighting supplied by Stage Electrics

With thanks to:

Mike Cordner
John Mullan
Tiffany Stern
Stella Tillyard
Betty Beesley at the Garrick Club
The Theatre Museum
Salisbury Playhouse

■ JERWOOD SPACE ■

**Creative &
Production
Teams**

April De Angelis (Writer of *A Laughing Matter*)
A Laughing Matter is April's second commission from Out of
Joint, following *The Positive Hour* which premiered in 1997
in a co-production with Hampstead Theatre. Other plays
for the **theatre** include *Ironmistress* (ReSisters Theatre co.);
The Life and Times of Fanny Hill (Red Shift); *Hush* (Royal
Court); *Soft Vengeance* (Graeae Theatre Company);
Playhouse Creatures (Old Vic Theatre & Sphinx Theatre
Company) and *The Warwickshire Testimony* (RSC). **Opera**
includes the libretto for *Flight* (Glyndebourne). April is
currently under commission from the Royal Court and the
RSC.

Oliver Goldsmith (Writer of *She Stoops to Conquer*)
Goldsmith was born in Pallas, County Longford, Ireland,
somewhere between 1728 and 1730. He studied medicine,
without great success, at the universities of Edinburgh,
Leyden and Padua before drifting into journalism. In 1760
he published *Chinese Letters*, a satire on contemporary
manners which soon established him as part of London's
literary set and as a friend of Dr Samuel Johnson. While his
first play, *The Good-Natured Man* (1768) was not popular,
his second, *She Stoops to Conquer*, premiered to critical
acclaim in 1773. It is said that the central misunderstanding
in the play is based on an event in Goldsmith's own life
when he mistook a gentleman's house for an inn. Other
literary works include the celebrated novel *The Vicar of
Wakefield* (1766) and the poem *The Deserted Village* (1770).
He died in 1774.

Stephen Jeffreys (Writer of Prologue and Epilogue for *She
Stoops to Conquer*)
Stephen has worked with Max Stafford-Clark on *The
Libertine* (Out of Joint 1994) and *A Jovial Crew* (RSC 1992)
and also wrote the prologue for *A Country Wife* (1993).
Valued Friends (Evening Standard Most Promising
Playwright Award 1989) and *A Going Concern* (1993) were
both hits at the Hampstead Theatre. His most recent plays
are *I Just Stopped By To See The Man* (Royal Court 2000)
and *Interruptions* (UC Davis, California 2001). *The Libertine*
was successfully presented by Steppenwolf in Chicago with
John Malkovich in the lead. A film version with Johnny
Depp goes into production this year.

Neil Alexander (Sound Designer)
This is Neil's first production for Out of Joint. Past **theatre**
productions include: *A Prayer for Owen Meany, Life After
Life, Vincent in Brixton, The Chain Play, Mother Clap's Molly
House, International Connections, Marriage Play / Finding
the Sun, Remembrance of Things Past, The Waiting Room,
Blue Orange, Sparkleshark* (National Theatre); *Observe the
Sons of Ulster* (Pleasance); *Moving On, Let's All Go to the
Fair, The Rough Road to Survival, Clubbed Out, Love Risk,*

*Don't Blame Her, Back to Back, Yard Gal, Been So Long,
Fair Game, Bailegangaire, Heredity* (Royal Court); *All
Manner of Means, Not Gods But Giants* (White Bear); *The
Snake House* (Greenwich Studio); *Shuffling Off, Northern
Lights* (New Grove); *Two Horsemen* (Gate / Bush); *The Year
of the Family* (Finborough); *Penetrator* (Traverse /
Finborough / RCT). **Film** work includes the short film
Private Dancer.

Wendy Allnutt (Choreographer)
Wendy has worked extensively as an actress including
West End, RSC, tours of USA, UK and Sweden. **TV**: *Sorry,
Dear John, The Regiment, The Bill*. **Films**: *Oh What a Lovely
War, When Eight Bells Toll* and *Priest of Love*.
Choreography: *Brothers Karamazov, Maybe* and *Private
Lives* (Manchester Royal Exchange); *India Song* (Clywd);
Goliath, Voyage in The Dark, A Wedding Story (Sphinx), and
most recently movement director on the forthcoming BBC
TV series *Walking with Cavemen*. Wendy is Head of
movement at the Guildhall School of Music and Drama.

William Conacher (Dialect Coach)
William's **theatre** work includes *The Blue Room*
(Haymarket); *Top Girls* (Aldwych); The Peter Gill Festival
(Crucible, Sheffield) and productions for the Chichester
Festival Theatre, the Royal Exchange, the Birmingham Rep
and the West Yorkshire Playhouse. **Film** work includes
Topsy Turvy, Three Blind Mice and *My Kingdom*. **Television**
includes *Faking It, Messiah, Dead Gorgeous* and *Celeb*.
William is also dialect coach at Rada.

Graham Cowley (Producer)
Out of Joint's Producer since 1998. His long collaboration
with Max Stafford-Clark began as Joint Stock Theatre
Group's first General Manager for seven years in the 1970s.
He was General Manager of the Royal Court for eight years,
and on their behalf transferred a string of hit plays to the
West End. His career has spanned the full range of theatre
production, from small fringe companies to major West End
shows and large scale commercial tours. Most recently
transferred the Royal Court's production of *The Weir* to the
West End, produced *A Kind of Alaska* at the Edinburgh
Festival and in the USA, and *Harry and Me* at the
Warehouse Theatre, Croydon.

Paddy Cunneen (Composer)
Paddy Cunneen first worked with Out of Joint on the score
for *Hinterland*. He has worked extensively as a composer
and music director in theatre throughout the UK and
Ireland. His work runs to well over 100 productions for the
RNT, RSC, Cheek By Jowl, Donmar Warehouse, Abbey,
Gate and Druid Theatres, Manchester Royal Exchange,
Royal Court, Liverpool Everyman and many others. In

addition he composes for BBC Radio Drama, RTE Radio Drama and has a number of TV and film credits. He is a recipient of the Christopher Whelen Award for Music in Theatre.

Julian McGowan (Designer)
For Out of Joint: *Feelgood* (Garrick); *The Steward of Christendom, Blue Heart, Shopping and Fucking* (with the Royal Court); *Some Explicit Polaroids, Our Country's Good* (with Young Vic), *Our Lady of Sligo* (with NT); *The Positive Hour* (with Hampstead). For the Royal Court: *Where Do We Live, I Just Stopped By to See the Man, Mr Kolpert, Toast, The Censor, American Bagpipes, The Treatment.* Other **theatre** includes: *Four Nights at Knaresborough* (New Vic Workshop at the Tricycle); *Enjoy, Blast From the Past, Waiting for Godot, Don Juan, The Lodger, Women Laughing* (Royal Exchange, Manchester); *The Possibilities, Venice Preserv'd, The LA Plays* (Almeida); *Heart Throb* (Bush); *The Wives' Excuse* (Royal Shakespeare Company); *Caesar and Cleopatra, Total Eclipse, A Tale of Two Cities* (Greenwich); *The Rivals, Man and Superman, Playboy of the Western World, Hedda Gabler.* **Opera** includes: *Cosi Fan Tutte* (New Israeli Opera); *Eugene Onegin* (Scottish Opera); *Siren Song* (Almeida Opera Festival).

Patsy Rodenburg (Company Voice Work)
Patsy Rodenburg trained at the Central School of Speech and Drama. She is Head of Voice at the National Theatre and Guildhall School of Music and Drama, and was voice tutor at the RSC for nine years. She works extensively in theatre, film, TV and radio throughout Europe, North America, Australia and Asia. She has given lessons to many of the world's leading theatre and opera companies, and maintains a continuous working relationship with Stratford Festival Theatre (Canada), Shared Experience, Cheek by Jowl, Theatre de Complicite, the Almeida Theatre, the Donmar Warehouse, the Royal Court Theatre, and Michael Howard Studio, New York. She is a Director of the Voice and Speech Centre, London. Publications: *The Right to Speak, The Need for Words* and *The Actor Speaks*, all published by Methuen. Video: *A Voice of Your Own.* Audio tape: *The Right to Speak.*

Max Stafford-Clark (Director)
Founded Joint Stock Theatre Group in 1974 following his Artistic Directorship of The Traverse Theatre, Edinburgh. From 1979 to 1993 he was Artistic Director of the Royal Court. In 1993 he founded Out of Joint. His work as a director has overwhelmingly been with new writing and he has commissioned and directed first productions by many of the country's leading writers.

Johanna Town (Lighting)

Johanna Town has worked on numerous Out of Joint productions including: *Hinterland, Rita, Sue and Bob Too / A State Affair, Some Explicit Polaroids, The Steward of Christendom, Shopping & Fucking, Our Lady of Sligo, Blue Heart* and *Feelgood*. She has been Head of Lighting at the Royal Court for the past twelve years and has lit **theatre** productions including: *The Kitchen, Faith Healer, Pale Horse, Search and Destroy, Women Laughing* and most recently: *Where Do We Live, Plasticine, Fucking Games, Nightingale & Chase, I Just Stopped By To See The Man, Spinning into Butter, Mr Kolpert* and *Under The Blue Sky*. Other recent theatre credits include: *Popcorn, Playboy of the Western World, Les Liasons Dangereuses* (Liverpool Playhouse); *She Stoops to Conquer* (Kent Opera); *Top Girls* (Oxford Stage Co / Aldwych West End); *Arabian Nights* (New Victory, New York); *Ghosts* (Royal Exchange Theatre); *Rose* (Lyceum Theatre, New York); *Little Malcolm and His Struggle Against the Eunuchs* (West End). **Opera** credits include: *Tobias & the Angel* (Almeida Opera festival); *La Boheme, Die Fledermaus, La Traviata,* (Music Theatre London); *Abduction from Seraglio, Marriage of Figaro* (Opera 80); *Marriage of Figaro, Otello* (Opera du Nice, France).

Matthew Wilde (Assistant Director)

Matthew previously assisted on the Out of Joint productions of *Hinterland* and the revival of the double bill *Rita, Sue and Bob Too / A State Affair*. He trained and studied at Bretton Hall, RADA & Kings College, London. As assistant director: *Camino Real, Twelfth Night, Sweet Bird of Youth* and *The Honest Whore* (RADA). As director theatre includes: *Criminals* (RNT Studio); *Stars in The Morning Sky* (Gielgud Theatre, RADA); *The Insatiate Countess* (Young Vic Studio Workshop); *Women Beware Women, Prometheus In Evin* and *Brighton Beach Scumbags* (Brockley Jack Theatre); *Romeo and Juliet, Macbeth* (Southwark Playhouse); *The Crucible* and *Vinegar Tom* (RADA at The Old Vic) and *Paradise* (Moray House Theatre, Edinburgh). Matthew is involved in developing and presenting new writing with writers from the Royal Court YWP, Goldsmith's College, RADA and the HOTBED Festival. He is also a member of the Readers' Panel at Soho Theatre and has worked extensively on various young people's theatre projects both in London and nationally, most recently with the English Shakespeare Company.

**Stephen Beresford
(Mr George Hastings** and **Edmund Burke / Sam Cautherley / Mr Cross)**
Trained at RADA. This is Stephen's third production for Out of Joint – he previously appeared in *Our Country's Good* and *Shopping and Fucking*. Other **theatre** work includes: *Free* (National Theatre); *Time and the Conways* (The Royal Exchange); *The Rivals* and *Rookery Nook* (Salisbury Playhouse); *Twelfth Night* (Liverpool Playhouse); *Woyzeck* (Gate Theatre); *Design for Living* (English Touring Theatre); *Charley's Aunt* and *French Without Tears* (Palace, Watford); *Woman in Mind* (Theatre Royal, York); *Dracula* (Everyman, Cheltenham) and a Chekhov workshop for the National Theatre Studio. **Film** and **tv** includes: *Casualty* and *History File* (BBC); *Where There's Smoke* (Talisman Films); *The Bill* (Thames); *Reunion* (Les Filmes Ariannes); *Spring Awakening* (RADA). **Radio** includes: *A Midsummer Night's Dream* and *As You Like It* for BBC Schools.

**Nigel Cooke
(Sir Charles Marlow** and **Charles Macklin / Sir Joshua Reynolds)**
Nigel last appeared with Out of Joint in *Feelgood*. Work with the Royal Shakespeare Company includes: *Macbeth* (Stratford / Tokyo), *Beckett's Shorts* (tour), *Pentecost, The Wives' Excuse, Henry V, School of Night, Volpone, Julius Caesar, Henry VIII* and *Twelfth Night*. His other **theatre** credits include: *All My Sons* (NT); *King Lear, The Recruiting Officer, Epsom Downs, The Three Musketeers* (Bristol Old Vic); *The Snow Palace* (Tricycle theatre); *The Iceman Cometh* (Almeida / Old Vic); *An Inspector Calls* and *Serious Money* (West End), *Suddenly Last Summer* (Haymarket Basingstoke); *Playboy of the Western World* (West Yorkshire Playhouse); *Romeo and Juliet* (Bolton Octagon); *The Public* (Stratford East); *The Duchess of Malfi* (Roundhouse); *Mere Soup Songs* and *Time and Time Again* (Scarborough); *Getting Attention, The Recruiting Officer* and *Our Country's Good* (Royal Court). **Television** includes: *Sons and Lovers, The Bill, Poirot, Silent Witness, Peak Practice VII, Casualty, Between the Lines, Hot Dog Wars, The Chief, Death of a Son, Galloping Galaxies* and *Why Lockerbie?*. **Film:** *Macbeth, I Just Want to Kiss You* and *Wesley – A Brand From the Burning*. He has also made numerous recordings for **Radio** 4.

**Monica Dolan
(Miss Kate Hardcastle** and **Peg Woffington/ Hannah Moore)**
Monica last appeared with Out of Joint in *Sliding with Suzanne* by Judy Upton. Other **theatre** includes: *The Glory of Living* (Royal Court); *The Walls* (NT); *The Taming of the Shrew, A Midsummer Night's Dream, Henry V, Coriolanus, Measure for Measure, Unfinished Business* (RSC); *Hay*

Fever (Savoy / West End); *An Experiment with an Air Pump* (Hampstead); *The Glass Menagerie* (Royal Lyceum, Edinburgh); *Jane Eyre* (Shared Experience tour / Young Vic); *Peter Pan* (West Yorkshire Playhouse); *Jane Eyre* (Theatre Royal, York); *To Kill a Mocking Bird* (Northcott Theatre); *Outside Edge, The Merchant of Venice* (Exeter). **Television** includes: *Tipping the Velvet* (Sally Head Productions); *Dalziel and Pascoe, Judge John Deed; Verdict – Rape* (BBC); *Screen One: The Gift* (Tetra Films); *The Bill* (Thames). **Film** includes: *Topsy Turvy* and *A Midsummer Night's Dream*.

Fritha Goodey
(Miss Constance Neville and **Mrs Garrick / Mrs Barry)**
Trained at LAMDA. This is Fritha's second production with Out of Joint – she previously appeared in Mark Ravenhill's *Some Explicit Polaroids*. Other **theatre** work includes: *Remembrance of Things Past* and *Romeo and Juliet* (RNT); *The Little French Lawyer, The Puritan, The Inn at Lydda* (Globe Theatre education). **Television** includes: *The Lost Prince* (Talkback); *A Case of Evil* (Box Films); *The Red Phone* (Atlas / Philos Films); *Hearts & Bones* and *Table Twelve* (World Productions); *Randall & Hopkirk Deceased* (Working Title TV); *Dr Willoughby* (Thames TV); *Roger Roger* (BBC). **Film** includes *About A Boy* for Boy Productions. **Radio** includes *After the Funeral* (BBC Radio) and *Pygmalion* (Naxos Audiobooks).

Bella Merlin
(Pimple and **Mrs Cibber)**
Following a degree in Drama and Theatre Arts at Birmingham University, Bella continued her training at Guildford School of Acting and The State Institute of Cinematography in Moscow. This is her second production with Out of Joint - she previously appeared in *The Queen and I*. Other **theatre** work includes *Anna Karenina* (Bolton Octagon); *Phil and Jill and Jill and Phil* (Coventry Belgrade / Swan Theatre, Worcester); *Ubu Rules!, Beauty and the Beast* (Orchard Theatre Co); *The Malvern Widow, Hard Times, Steaming, Can't Pay? Won't Pay!, The Turn of the Screw, The Seagull* (Swan Theatre, Worcester); *Orlando* (Lyric Hammersmith and Red Shift tour); *Lulu* (Chelsea Centre Theatre); *Brighton Beach Memoirs,* and *The Cat and the Canary* (Haymarket, Basingstoke). **Television** includes *Doctors, Acting With...* (BBC) and *The Empress* (Channel 4). She recently recorded Lucy Gough's acclaimed *The Raft* (Radio 4). Bella is also a Lecturer in Drama and Theatre Arts at Birmingham University, with publications including *Beyond Stanislavsky: The Psycho-Physical Approach to Actor-Training* (Nick Hern Books) and the forthcoming *Stanislavsky* (Routledge). She performed in her first play, *Hit*, alongside collaborator, Alexander Delamere, at the Octagon, Bolton.

Ian Redford
(Mr Hardcastle and **Dr Samuel Johnson / Rev.**
Cumberland / Betty Flint)
This is Ian's fifth appearance with Out of Joint – previous
productions include *Rita, Sue and Bob Too / A State Affair;*
Some Explicit Polaroids, Shopping and Fucking and *Our
Country's Good.* Other **theatre** includes: Princess
Seraphina in *Mother Clap's Molly House* and *Free* (NT);
Built on Sand; Bruises (Royal Court). He has worked in
most theatres in the country in productions including: *Tiger
Tail* (Drum Theatre, Plymouth); *Agamemnon's Children*
(Gate Theatre); *'M' Butterfly* (Shaftesbury Theatre); *Chapter
Two* (Gielgud Theatre and Theatre Royal, Windsor); *Hamlet*
(Chester Gateway Theatre). **Television** includes: *Lovejoy;
Coronation Street; EastEnders; Wycliffe and Animal Ark.* Ian
also played 'Larry Cotter' in *House of Eliott* and 'Jimmy
Plinth' in *September Song.* Recent **television** work
includes Who Killed Ruth Ellis; Peak Practice; Second Sight
and *Trial by Fire.* **Film** includes: *Remains of the Day;
Getting it Right; Just Like a Woman; Stone Scissors Paper;
Three Men and a Little Lady; Orphan Annie; The Prince and
the Pauper.*

Owen Sharpe
(Tony Lumpkin and **Oliver Goldsmith / Theophilus**
O'Ryan)
This is Owen's first appearance with Out of Joint. Previous
theatre includes: *The Lieutenant of Inishmore, Jubilee,
Shadows, Purgatory, Bartholomew Fair, The Lime Tree
Bower* (RSC); *The Cripple of Inishmaan* and *Pericles* (NT);
*The Barbaric Comedies, Mrs Warren's Profession,
Macbeth, Madigan's Lock* and *A Thief of Christmas* (The
Abbey); *Brighton Beach Memoirs* and *Billy Liar* (Andrews
Lane Theatre); *Jacko* (Hawks Well Theatre); *Bugsy Malone*
(Olympia Theatre); *Dear Jack* (The Ark). **Television**
includes: *The Favourite, Crime Line, The Lolly Man, My
Oedipus Complex, Deco* and *A Summer Ghost.* **Film**
includes: *Borstal Boys, Leprechaun* and *My Left Foot.*

Matthew Sim
(Landlord / Jeremy and **Cedric Bounce / Mr Larpent)**
Trained at LAMDA and the National Youth Theatre. This is
Matthew's first production with Out of Joint. Previous
theatre work includes: *School for Scandal* (Derby &
Northampton); *Merlin* (Riverside Studios); *Highway to
Paradise* (Arte Del Teatro Studio, Rome); *Three Sisters*
(Chichester Festival); *The Impressario from Smyrna* (Old
Red Lion); *Twelfth Night* (Drill Hall); *The Lost Domain*
based on *Le Grand Meaulnes* (Watermill, Newbury); *The
Royal Hunt of the Sun* (Compass Theatre); *A Little Hotel on
the Side, Mandragola, Saint Joan* (NT); *Dealing with Clair*
(Orange Tree); *Charley's Aunt* (Southwold); *Arcade* (Loose
Exchange); *Children of the Wolf* (Royal Northampton);

Class Enemy (Library Manchester); *Peter Pan* (Crucible, Sheffield); *Richard III* (RSC); *The Two Noble Kinsmen* (Cherub Theatre Co.). **Film** includes: *Gangs of New York, Ancient Warriors, The Emperor's New Clothes, In the Beginning, The Hunchback of Notre Dame, Interview with a Vampire, Orlando, Without a Clue, Revolution, Maurice, Lionheart, An Englishman Abroad, Scum* the short films *Laws of Motion, Before I Die Forever* and *Straightforward Kenneth,* and music videos for Moby and Goldie. **Television** includes: *Border Café, Monster TV, Middlemarch, Clarissa; Let Them Eat Cake; Alice in Wonderland; A Dance to the Music of Time; Full Stretch ; The Young Indiana Jones Chronicles.* He was also a member of the BBC **Radio** Drama Company from 1991-1992.

Christopher Staines
(Young Charles Marlow and **James Boswell / Mr Barry / Duke of Kingston)**
This is Christopher's first production for Out of Joint. Previous **theatre** includes: for the National, *Hamlet* and *Amy's View* (also in the West End); *Silence* (Birmingham Rep); *Three Sisters* (Chichester Festival Theatre); *Gross Indecency - The Three Trials of Oscar Wilde* (Theatre Royal Plymouth and West End); *Leonce and Lena* (The Gate Theatre); *The Belle Vue* (ATC); *A Midsummer Night's Dream, Richard III, The Music Man* (Regent's Park); *The Simpleton of the Unexpected Isles, The Memorandum, Portrait of a Woman, Flora the Red Menace* (Orange Tree Theatre); *Cabaret* (Donmar Warehouse); *An Evening with Gary Lineker* (Royal Theatre, Northampton). **Television** includes: *The Student Prince, This Life, The Queen's Nose, Pride and Prejudice, Highlander, The Ruby Ring, Good Friday 1663.* **Film** includes: *Mrs Dalloway.* **Radio** includes: *Dossier Ronald Akkerman, The Rose and the Ring, The Charm Factory, The Decameron* and *Antigone.*

Jason Watkins
(Diggory and **David Garrick)**
This is Jason's third appearance with Out of Joint – previous productions include *Blue Heart* and *Man of Mode / Libertine.* Other **theatre** work includes: *Bedroom Farce* (Aldwych Theatre); *Boy Gets Girl, King Lear, Rafts and Dreams* (Royal Court); *A Servant to Two Masters* (RSC, Young Vic, New Ambassadors, World Tour, Albery Theatres) for which he received an Olivier Award nomination and the Helen Hayes Award for Best Actor in the United States; *Kissing the Pope, Plantagenets, The Plain Dealer* (RSC); *Kafka's Dick, Filumena* (Piccadilly Theatre); *After Darwin* (Hampstead Theatre); *A Midummer Night's Dream* (Almeida); *Habeus Corpus* (Donmar); *My Night with Reg* (Criterion & Playhouse Theatres); *One Flea Spare, Keyboard Skills* (Bush Theatre); *A Handful of Dust*

(Cambridge Theatre Co); *Inadmissable Evidence* (NT); *The House of Yes* (Gate); *The Rivals* (Nottingham Playhouse), *True West, The Government Inspector, As you Like It* (Crucible Sheffield); *Timon of Athens* (Young Vic); *Jack the Giant* (Royal Exchange, Manchester). **Television** includes: *Saving Grace; The Russian Bride* (ITV); *Sex 'N' Death* (Hatrick); *Couples, Bostocks Cup, Duck Patrol, Good Guys* (LWT); *Grown Ups, Casualty, Between the Lines, Buddha of Suburbia, Pie in the Sky* (BBC), *Soldier, Soldier* (Central). **Film** includes: *Sabotage, Tomorrow Never Dies, Circus, Eugene Onegin, High Hopes, Split Second*.

Jane Wood
(Mrs Hardcastle and **Lady Kingston / Mrs Butler)**
This is Jane's third appearance with Out of Joint – previous productions include *The Queen and I* and the double bill *Rita, Sue and Bob Too / A State Affair*. Other **theatre** work includes: *Mrs Steinberg & the Byker Boy* and *Fosdyke Saga* (Bush Theatre); *The Entertainer, This Story of Yours, Comings & Goings* (Hampstead Theatre); *Eve of Retirement* (Gate Theatre); *Tulip Futures* (Soho Theatre Co.); *The Project* (Soho Poly); *Don Quixote* (National Theatre); *Gorky Brigade and Live Like Pigs* (Royal Court); *Devils Island, Epsom Downs, A Mad World My Masters* (Joint Stock); *The Prisoner's Pumpkin* and *To* (Bristol Old Vic); *Hated Nightfall* (Wrestling School); *Nice Girls* (New Vic, Stoke); *Deadwood* (Watermill, Newbury). **Television** credits include: *Shipman, Impact; Railway Children; First and Last; Precious Bane; The Monocled Mutineer; The Russian Soldier; Good as Gold; Ball Trap on the Côte Sauvage; A Time to Dance; Darling Buds of May; House of Elliott; Bramwell; Casualty; The Bill; Heartbeat; Peak Practice; A Wing and a Prayer; City Central; Midsomer Murders*. **Film** credits include: *Persuasion; Smack and Thistle; Raggedy Rawney; She'll be Wearing Pink Pyjamas; Sakharov; The Ragman's Daughter*.

Both David Garrick and Samuel Johnson came from the Staffordshire Cathedral city of Lichfield. We rehearsed there for a week and although April De Angelis' play *A Laughing Matter* chronicles the disagreements between Goldsmith and Garrick, they ended as friends. We have imagined that this production of *She Stoops To Conquer* is set in the hinterland of Lichfield. I hope Dr Goldsmith would have approved.

Max Stafford-Clark

April De Angelis
A Laughing Matter

faber and faber

First published in 2002
by Faber and Faber Limited
3 Queen Square, London WC1N 3AU

Typeset by Country Setting, Kingsdown, Kent CT14 8ES
Printed in England by Mackays of Chatham plc, Chatham, Kent

A CIP record for this book
is available from the British Library

ISBN 0-571-21772-9

2 4 6 8 10 9 7 5 3 1

Characters

Samuel Johnson
Oliver Goldsmith
James Boswell
Edmund Burke
Joshua Reynolds
David Garrick
Mrs Eva Garrick
Lady Kingston
Reverend Richard Cumberland
Sam Cautherley
Mrs Susannah Cibber
Mrs Butler
Mrs Lavinia Barry
Mr Spranger Barry
Mr Charles Macklin
Hannah More
Cedric Bounce
Mr Richard Cross
Master Barry
Mr Theophilus O'Ryan
Peg Woffington
Betty Flint
Duke of Kingston
Old Man
Butcher
Vicar
Mr Larpent

Act One

Johnson A Club. 1. An assembly of good fellows meeting under certain conditions for a common purpose. 2. A heavy tapering stick, knobby at one end. Used to strike with.

SCENE ONE: THE TURK'S HEAD

In which eminent men discuss the nature of contemporary theatre.

Goldsmith Gentlemen, I have written a comedy, but when or how it will be acted or whether it will be acted at all are questions I cannot resolve.

Boswell Gentlemen, we forget our toast. To the Turk's Head.

All The Turk's Head!

Johnson I find I no longer approve of our toast. We are not Turks. We must endeavour to discover a more suitable epithet.

Goldsmith Gentlemen. May I draw attention to the matter I flagged up some moments past?

Johnson No, Goldy, you may not. You must not be forever attempting to shine in conversation. You go on without ever knowing how you are to get off. You seldom come anywhere where you are not more ignorant than anyone else.

Burke If I remember correctly, Dr Johnson's pledge of old was to the king over the water.

Johnson It was, Mr Burke, until he threatened to arrive.

Burke You had not the stomach to be overrun by marauding Scots?

Johnson Scots, sir, will grab the flimsiest of straws to leave the land of their birth. Invasion of England would merely have provided them further excuse.

Boswell You are rather harsh upon my country fellows, I think.

Johnson A man cannot admire a nation whose national dish is oats. Oats in England, sir, are a cereal fed to horses. In Scotland they support the population. You may enquire of Reynolds here as to landscape.

Reynolds The landscape is perhaps a trifle severe for the English palette.

Johnson Just as your eye is blighted, so is the mind, for conversation has not yet been invented in Scotland. They are too busy chewing.

Boswell I object, sir.

Johnson You may object, Bozzy, or you may comfort yourself with this: although it is bad to be Scottish it is worse to be French. The French are a gross, ill-bred, untaught people; a lady there will spit on the floor and rub it with her foot.

Burke If we are to discover for ourselves a new pledge, we must go back to first principles. Why are we here?

Johnson Burke is the man, sirs, take up whatever topic you please, he is ready to meet you. We meet here to advance the cause of learning and furnish through our conversation understanding and enlightened thinking. We are at the helm, sirs, of an English renaissance. Which brings me to my matter.

Goldsmith Which brings me to my matter.

Johnson I have not finished, sir.

Goldsmith In essence.

Johnson Have I not shaken you off yet, Goldy? My point is this: that our toast, sirs, should be to England.

All England.

Goldsmith My point is that Mr Colman at Covent Garden has had my play twenty-two months. And, sirs, since I have been living off the expectation of it being performed, I am now brought so low as to face extinction. L–l–look at me one last time. I am a whisker away from the slab. Last night I ate my candle then lay in the darkness knowing my final hour must be approaching. Alas, this morning I woke as usual.

Boswell But what is your point, sir?

Johnson His point is he has no candle.

Reynolds You must apply to me for candles, sir. I shall furnish you gladly.

Boswell Perhaps your play is no good, sir.

Goldsmith I have examined all possibilities and that is the least probable. The truth is that your renaissance, sirs, has by-passed the English theatre altogether. We have no theatre to speak of.

Boswell That's odd. I could've sworn I was there last night.

Goldsmith What we have is a commercial venture. A different matter altogether.

Burke Now see here, Dr Goldsmith, we cannot allow you to cast aspersions upon commercial ventures – they are an expression of man's interests.

Reynolds It says something for a work of art that a man is prepared to pay for it.

Goldsmith If you are prepared to flatter, sir, men will pay you.

Boswell Ooh!

Johnson Now, Goldy . . .

Reynolds I flatter myself that I like to bring out the best in people.

Boswell Indeed you do, sir. I say that without flattery.

Johnson Knowing you as I do, Bozzy, that is highly improbable.

Burke Do you suggest Sir Joshua bring out the worst in his subjects?

Johnson It is reasonable to suppose that a man may desire to be presented in a good light as opposed to a bad.

Burke If it makes him content, should we not be happy for him?

Goldsmith It is not the b–business of art to content a man with his own flaws!

Reynolds You touch upon a philosophic point. Shouldn't art aspire to the ideal, since beauty instructs us in goodness?

Burke We would not wish to return to the barbaric impulses which lie within man's breast by always harking on his beastliness.

Goldsmith But it is a lie . . . gentlemen. An argument for lying.

Boswell A society must be encouraged in its aspirations.

Goldsmith I contend that the theatre, sir, is . . .

Johnson The theatre, I am not for it. A man is better off reading a play in the comfort of his own home.

Goldsmith You give yourself no concern about new p–plays as if you never had a thing to do with the stage. B–but you wrote a p–play once.

All *Irene.*

They giggle.

Johnson And the Sultan Mahomet. The theatre , sir, is a pointless activity. What does it benefit a man to sit squashed in unspeakable circumstances watching another prance and gesticulate upon a stage in clothes not his own? What does it give a man but a sore arse! A man of talent may do no better than leave the theatre well alone.

Goldsmith Gentlemen . . . I am reduced to eating my only source of lighting. Until I am assisted I will beat myself about the head with this book, the first volume of my own *Deserted Village*. (*He does so.*)

Boswell What is he about, Doctor?

Johnson Sir, the conversation overflowed and drowned him.

Reynolds Dr Goldsmith, please refrain. This is hardly the behaviour of a gentleman.

Johnson Goldy, you cannot treat books in that manner.

Burke Stop, sir, or I will be forced to set about you with my stick. (*He stops.*)

Goldsmith That's a b–big stick.

Johnson Have you not thought, Goldy, of taking your play to Mr Garrick? For if Mr Colman at Covent

Garden will not have it, then perhaps his rival at Drury Lane may be persuaded.

Burke Excellent, Doctor.

Boswell You have hit upon it.

Reynolds A most satisfactory conclusion.

Goldsmith Garrick! Never!

Reynolds There's no pleasing Dr Goldsmith.

Burke What have you against Mr Garrick?

Goldsmith He is a scoundrel.

Johnson Garrick is a dear friend. Only I may disparage him.

Boswell Garrick is the greatest actor that has ever lived.

Goldsmith He has single-handedly destroyed the English theatre.

Burke I disagree, sir. By fine and considered management Garrick has saved our theatre from extinction.

Reynolds Garrick may be commended with rescuing Shakespeare from obscurity.

Johnson Sir, you lampoon the age. Some of us had acquaintance with him already.

Goldsmith But what of new plays! Is the credit of our own age nothing? Must our own time pass away unnoticed by posterity?

Reynolds I have painted Mr Garrick on two occasions. He doesn't stay in one expression long. The longer I painted him the further away I got. His face was best as a cloud.

Johnson What is a player but a shadow, sir?

Goldsmith A substantial shadow! P–puffed up with vanity.

Johnson No wonder, sir, that he is vain. A man who has a nation to admire him every night may well be expected to be somewhat elated.

Goldsmith But he turned down my first play and I wrote bad things about him.

Johnson Do you need me to come along and hold your hand, Goldy?

Goldsmith Yes p–please. I should like a b–big thing beside me.

Johnson Very well. Now let us call an end to the matter. I have no desire to extend it further. I should rather hear Bozzy whistle a Scotch tune.

Burke I propose a discussion on the nature of art.

Boswell All societies have art.

Johnson No, sir, some have pottery.

SCENE TWO: GARRICK'S OFFICE

Garrick performs for Mrs Garrick.

Garrick
Give me another horse! Bind up my wounds!
Have mercy, Jesu!

At this point he operates a mechanism in his wig and his hair stands on end.

Soft, I did but dream.
Oh coward conscience, how thou dost affect me.

His hair subsides.

Even his wig can act.

11

Mrs Garrick Bravo, Mr Garrick.

Garrick You've seen it before, Mrs Garrick.

Mrs Garrick And it always alarms me. It's almost time for your ten o'clock. How will you be?

Garrick 'Surprised at work', I think. Don't you?

Mrs Garrick That or 'actor muses by bookcase'.

Garrick I could do 'actor extremely surprised by visit'. (*He operates his wig in imitation of shock/horror.*) I suppose you'll be in the cupboard.

Mrs Garrick Of course!

Garrick You've spent quite a lot of time in there. It's only five-by-five. I feel quite bad about it.

Mrs Garrick Mr Garrick. What's got into you? I enjoy it. They'll be here.

Garrick (*taking a studious pose.*) Time's gone much quicker than I ever imagined.

Mrs Garrick What's the matter?

Garrick Nothing. We've had the most wonderful life. I just liked it when the end felt a long way off.

Mrs Garrick gives him a pat. They hear an approaching entrance. She goes into the secret cupboard. A second later she comes out.

Lady Kingston (*off*) Mr Garrick.

Mrs Garrick Wig!

Garrick quickly takes off mechanical wig and puts on proper one. Mrs Garrick vanishes. Lady Kingston sweeps in, followed by Reverend Cumberland.

Lady Kingston Mr Garrick. Genius and national treasure!

Garrick acts his 'surprised at work'. He then leaps to his feet and bows.

Garrick Lady Kingston, I'm honoured.

Lady Kingston So this is your office?

Garrick Your Grace.

Lady Kingston It's absolutely charming. You know Reverend Cumberland?

Garrick Very well. How do you do, sir?

Cumberland Pleased to meet you again, sir.

Lady Kingston Well this is delightful. Now we saw your Lear last season and it was quite tremendous, Mr Garrick.

Garrick Thank you.

Lady Kingston It really was.

Garrick Thank you.

Lady Kingston And we've just been talking about it ever since. And it's so much better with your ending.

Garrick Thank you.

Lady Kingston The original is so depressing and may encourage people to hang their relatives.

Cumberland Her Ladyship was saying that your power to move was simply remarkable.

Lady Kingston Yes, I was. May I speak frankly? My husband, the Duke, is a good deal older than I and is in politics. Just recently I've felt a certain languor. Apprehending his complete indifference, I turned for solace to our parson who, it transpired, has written a play. My first thoughts upon the matter were, I must admit, what utter tedium. But Reverend Cumberland soon impressed upon me the very serious nature of such an enterprise. It is extraordinary, all these clergymen writing plays – you must be delighted.

Garrick I'm ecstatic.

Lady Kingston And it keeps them away from religion, which has led to so much trouble in the past. I'm so keen to get involved, Mr Garrick. The Reverend Cumberland has written a new weeping comedy called . . .

Cumberland *The Fashionable Lover.*

Lady Kingston *The Fashionable Lover.*

Cumberland It has no jokes in it.

Garrick Yes, I know. Reverend Cumberland kindly sent it me.

Lady Kingston This is what's so wonderful about what's happening in the theatre at the moment. There's a real sense of purpose.

Cumberland While weeping comedy has gained considerable ground on our stages, elevating tears above humour, it can go further. What is laughter but the wilful enjoyment of the misfortunes of others?

Lady Kingston And the forcible expulsion of air from the larynx.

Cumberland You laugh *at* people but you cry *with* them. Laughter divides us. Tears draw us together.

Lady Kingston I take culture very seriously. It is one field in which a woman may exert an influence and in so doing restore a reputation somewhat sullied by incessant gambling. The present Royals are sticklers for reputation. Do make use of me.

Garrick The theatre is always grateful of a presence such as yours, Lady Kingston.

Lady Kingston Mr Garrick, through a spotless reputation you've raised your profession to respectability. It has seen you admitted to the greatest houses in the land.

Garrick I have been most fortunate . . .

Lady Kingston You have. You must bring yourself and Mrs Garrick to Chatham. There's very good shooting.

Garrick I'm overwhelmingly flattered, ma'am.

Lady Kingston There's a revolution taking place in our country concerning polite behaviour. We can't just carry on as we did in the past. Table manners were appalling. My father-in-law once consumed half a pig and he didn't use cutlery.

Garrick Your Grace.

Cumberland I expect I'll be hearing news of my play shortly?

Garrick Drury Lane does produce one new play each season, Your Grace. We produced the Reverend's *The West Indian* two seasons past. It enjoyed considerable success.

Lady Kingston Excellent, Mr Garrick. Can I ask one more favour? A recitation?

Garrick Your Grace.

Garrick poses. He does an extract from Macbeth. *A stunning alteration. A very physical performance of a death scene.*

Before my body
I throw my warlike shield: lay on Macduff,
And damn'd be him that first cries hold enough!
'Tis done! The scene of life will quickly close.
Ambition's vain, delusive dreams are fled.
And now I wake to darkness, guilt and horror.

I cannot bear it! Let me shake it off.
Twa' not be; my soul is clogged with blood,
I cannot rise! I dare not ask for mercy.
It is too late, hell drags me down. I sink,
I sink . . . oh! . . . my soul is lost for ever! . . . Oh!

He dies.
   A pause.
   Lady Kingston is moved.

Lady Kingston And you wrote that yourself, Mr Garrick. Marvellous.

Garrick A small addition to the original.

Cumberland Providing a welcome sense of moral repentance.

Lady Kingston And the writhing is most affecting. Good day.

She exits, followed by Cumberland. Garrick is still a moment – to ensure that they have gone – then he appears to double up in pain. Mrs Garrick rushes out of the cupboard.

Mrs Garrick You would do that one!

She takes some smelling salts out of the bag at her waist and gives them to Garrick. At that point Cumberland re-enters. Mrs Garrick disappears. Garrick straightens up.

Cumberland Could I alert you to a small change I've made on page 147? I've substituted the word 'fourpenny-worth' for 'a shilling'.

Garrick Yes, yes, yes. Thank you, Cumberland.

Cumberland She's a very forceful woman, Mr Garrick.

Garrick Yes, I can see that. Good day.

Cumberland exits. Garrick, in some agony, sits down. Mrs Garrick reappears.

Mrs Garrick Did they even mention if there's a part for you in it?

She opens a drawer in his desk, takes out some medicine and spoons some out for him. He takes it.

Garrick Chatham, Mrs Garrick. Forty-six bedrooms and three French chefs. She owns Surrey.

Mrs Garrick Open up, Mr Garrick. (*She gives him more medicine. She then puts it away.*) I'm very glad we're retiring.

Garrick I've still a season to go, Mrs Garrick, don't rush me. (*He walks around as if to prove he's not suffering. A slight limp.*) I'm not too bad. (*He imitates Cumberland.*) I've substituted the word 'fourpennyworth' for 'a shilling'. (*as himself*) His plays would be nothing much if we didn't spruce them up a bit.

A knock at the door.

Mrs Garrick But I expect there'll be a part for Sam in this one.

They quickly put away medicine. Garrick composes himself. Mrs Garrick hands him a play. He appears to be perusing it. Mrs Garrick disappears.

Garrick Come in.

Sam Cautherley enters.

Cautherley Mr Garrick.

He holds out his hand. Garrick springs into action.

Garrick Mr Cautherley. (*He shakes his hand.*) You appear to have grown a few inches since the last time we met.

Cautherley I may have, sir.

Garrick Welcome home.

Cautherley Thank you, sir.

Garrick So you've seen a few great cities on your trip?

Cautherley Yes, sir.

Garrick What did you think to them?

Cautherley I liked them.

Garrick Rome, Vienna, Paris. Quite something for a young man.

Cautherley Yes, and I'd like to take this opportunity of thanking you, sir.

Garrick Well, a young gentleman isn't a gentleman these days unless he's been on his tour. Show me something, Mr Cautherley.

Cautherley I beg your pardon?

Garrick You must have seen something of interest?

Cautherley I bought you some artistic reproductions of the major sights.

Garrick No, no, no. I meant something particular you've observed. Actors are great observers of life, Mr Cautherley.

Cautherley I see. There were things I noted.

Garrick I should hope so – you've been gone a year.

Cautherley The cry of the fishwives at Dover. It sounded like one long wail. (*He demonstrates.*) Apparently they're saying, 'Half a pound of mussels straight out the pond.'

Garrick That's not the kind of thing I meant at all. If you're going to become an actor, I doubt you'll be playing a fishwife.

Cautherley An actor?

Garrick Not unless you're very disappointing. Think again, Mr Cautherley. Didn't you see anything useful?

Cautherley I did observe in Paris, among the gentlemen, that one glove only is removed and laid transversely across the knee, like so. (*He demonstrates.*)

Garrick Excellent, excellent. Mrs Garrick will be delighted.

Mrs Garrick enters from secret room.

Mrs Garrick Sam. (*She embraces him.*)

Cautherley Mrs Garrick!

Garrick My wife has spent twenty-six years eavesdropping in the interests of the English theatre. I'm sure you won't hold it against her.

Mrs Garrick It was all in a good cause.

Garrick Show her that thing with the glove.

Sam demonstrates.

Good, isn't it?

Mrs Garrick (*to Sam*) Wonderful. Because, you know, he's not as strong as he used to be.

Garrick Now, Mrs Garrick.

Mrs Garrick It's true, Davy. (*to Sam*) He suffers with the stone and I'm up all night with him and it takes ages to pass one. Little rocks. Awful.

Garrick Does he really have to know all this, Eva?

Mrs Garrick gets one of the rocks out from her handkerchief in her bag. She hands it to Cautherley . . .

Mrs Garrick Look. Really it is a rock.

. . . who can hardly bear to hold it but manages through politeness.

Cautherley Ah, yes.

Garrick No, no, no. (*Garrick retrieves the stone and gives it back to Mrs Garrick.*) Put it away, Eva.

Mrs Garrick (*to Sam*) Bent double. That is why it's so good you've come. To take some of the weight off his shoulders.

Garrick You're jumping the gun, Mrs Garrick. Now we've always said you had the makings of an actor. That's why I gave you lessons in the school holidays.

Cautherley I wish I was able to express my gratitude for the interest you've always taken in my welfare.

Garrick We were happy to do so, Sam. We had no children of our own.

Mrs Garrick You know the theatre is now a respectable profession for a gentleman.

Cautherley Yes, I know.

Mrs Garrick And it wasn't like that when we started out. It was a rake's paradise. Men would jump on stage and ravage a cleavage. Davy put a stop to that.

Garrick It spoiled the dramatic illusion. I've nothing against cleavages *per se*.

Mrs Garrick People aren't afraid to bring their daughters now. And daughters have as much right to a night out as anyone.

Garrick And then we sell more tickets. You see, the ladies will like you.

Cautherley Well, I don't know.

Garrick Don't be modest, Sam, they like a pretty face.

Mrs Garrick And a handsome figure.

Garrick You see, he's got the eyes. If it's one thing I had from nature it was the eyes.

Cautherley I just can't see myself being an actor, sir.

  Pause.

Garrick Why not? It's a profession that can bring great rewards.

Mrs Garrick Mr Garrick came from nothing. Look at him now.

Garrick Not quite nothing, Eva.

Mrs Garrick Soldiers. My father was an Austrian cunt.

Garrick (*correcting her pronunciation*) Count, Eva.

Cautherley I have been privileged to witness your genius, Mr Garrick. Your power to move and to terrify, to bring to life the greatest sentiments of the poets . . .

Garrick That's well said, Mrs Garrick.

Cautherley I could never get anywhere near that, Mr Garrick.

Garrick I've reason to believe you would be exceptional, Mr Cautherley.

  Pause.

But as you wish. (*He gets up to shake Cautherley's hand. As he does so, he pitches forward onto his desk in an attack of the stone.*)

Cautherley Mr Garrick.

Garrick (*writing*) Good day, Mr Cautherley!

Cautherley Can't something be done?

Mrs Garrick Nothing, I'm afraid.

Garrick does an elaborate show of it. It subsides.

Cautherley Mr Garrick, I had no idea. Of course, if you think I have the potential to be an actor, then I will give it my very best shot.

Garrick Welcome to Drury Lane, sir.

They shake hands.

Mrs Garrick I'll show you out, Sam.

Garrick (*calls*) We open Monday week!

Mrs Garrick shuts the door behind Sam. Garrick as normal.

Very fine eyes.

Mrs Garrick stands as if protecting the door.

Mrs Garrick You've two more visitors, Mr Garrick. You've had quite a morning. Shall I ask them to come back tomorrow?

Garrick Who are they?

Mrs Garrick Dr Johnson and the other one. A writer. I think there's something moving in his wig.

Garrick I can't turn away Dr Johnson, we would never hear the end of it.

She shows them in.

Mrs Garrick I have something for you, Doctor.

Johnson Ma'am.

She leaves. Garrick poses himself holding a wooden box which he has on his desk.

Garrick Dr Johnson. Dr Goldsmith. What an unexpected pleasure.

Johnson Davy.

Garrick holds up the box.

Garrick You've caught me strolling down memory lane. May I show you? But perhaps you're not interested.

Johnson It has something curious inside it?

Garrick Nothing. But it may amuse you. It is carved around with figures. Macbeth, Hamlet, Lear. The citizens of Stratford saw fit to present it to me.

Johnson It is a box, sir. A reasonable man knows the value of proportion. I have written extensively on Shakespeare and am happy to say I was never rewarded with woodcrafts. We come to see you on an urgent matter.

Goldsmith My p–play. *She Stoops to Conquer, or The Mistakes of a Night.*

Johnson Dr Goldsmith is very poor and no one will put on his play so we have brought it to you.

Garrick That was very good of you.

Goldsmith Last week I ate my candle.

Garrick Is that the sort of thing that goes on in your play?

Goldsmith No, that wouldn't b–be funny.

Garrick Oh, I don't know.

Johnson Give him the play, Goldy.

Goldsmith does so.

Goldsmith The address of my lodgings is on the front.

Johnson Dr Goldsmith is a man of considerable talent although to look at him he appears something lunatic.

Goldsmith Thank you. I am horrible. I am forced into hack work; writing the *Animated History of Nature* in twenty-seven volumes. Did you know b–by the b–by that the great B–British Diving B-Beetle may b–be categorised as b–both a fish and a b–beetle. I'm forty-five. I remain a virgin. My great knowledge of its flora and fauna has failed to impress the women of B–Britain. My face continues to appal me. I have an eye disgustingly severe and a b–big wig. I by no means wish any of this to influence your decision on my play.

Garrick No, that would be unprofessional.

Johnson As you can see, Goldy's case is pressing. His play must go on as soon as possible.

Garrick Mr Colman has been considering it for Covent Garden I believe. What reasons does he give for hesitating?

Goldsmith He says it is low.

Garrick Is it?

Goldsmith It is funny, Mr Garrick. That, upon occasion, requires a little lowness!

Johnson You must explain the play a little, Goldy. Whet Davy's appetite for the thing. You must not be always twitching and shouting.

Goldsmith Very well. The hero Marlow is an idiot based on myself. He mistakenly believes he is staying at an inn and not the house of his father's oldest friend. There he tries to have his way with a barmaid.

Garrick Good Lord!

Goldsmith Don't worry – she's really the daughter of the house disguised as a barmaid.

Garrick That's worse, isn't it?

Goldsmith Marlow can't be honest with women of his own station – the curse of the middling sort – that is why Kate disguises herself – she stoops to conquer. Oh, and then there's Tony Lumpkin – the son. A wild, mischievous creature who really is . . . with a barmaid!

Garrick I'm not surprised at Colman's hesitation, Doctor. This play sounds as inflammatory as the last one. An audience likes to see moral flaws punished, not laughed at.

Goldsmith That's sentimental bollocks. It doesn't do the job that comedy does to p–point out our p–pomposity and hyp–pocrisy. It's sentimental bollocks! Good Lord – I'm the worst of the lot. I've fine clothes I can't afford – affectations of being a great writer when I've hardly tuppence to rub together. I see them whisper about me . . . my tight trousers and my monkey face. If I didn't laugh at myself . . . I'd be a madman.

Johnson Well said, Goldy.

Garrick I thought you'd grown disenchanted with the theatre, sir.

Johnson I have. I had hopes of it once, but they all came to nothing.

Garrick You are severe.

Johnson On the contrary, sir, I am mild considering the state of the art.

Garrick Well, since you never come, sir, it is very ingenious of you to be able to judge.

Johnson I have come enough, sir, to know that I had best keep away.

Garrick One wonders why you seek to promote your friend here.

Johnson Because he is my friend, sir. We come to you, Davy, because you've had a deal of success and can afford to be generous.

Garrick Thank you, I do credit myself with some modest success.

Johnson You are an actor, sir, let us remember. We may pass a pleasant half-hour with Mr Punch, but to reward him with a town house, another in the country and all with fine furniture beggars belief. There are others engaged in serious work who can barely scratch up a supper.

Garrick You must know, Dr Goldsmith, that Dr Johnson was once my schoolmaster and he has never quite lost that way with me. Let me run a few figures past you. Drury Lane. Twelve boxes, five shillings each. Pit, 450 seats. Prices range from three shillings to two shillings six pence. Upper Gallery, 250 seats. A shilling each. A full house may make in revenue £375 a night. Now bear in mind that Drury Lane employs over one hundred and eighty musicians, stagehands, actors. On top of that there is the general cost of running a building. There are invisible costs – we are suffering litigation as I speak from a young lady who was struck on the head by a lump of hard cheese dropped on her from the upper gallery. Profit margins are slimmer than might first appear. If a play gets a bad smell we certainly feel the pinch. Two in a row and we court disaster. And there are those, sir, who as in the past, would not shed a tear to see us go. I have a responsibility to my theatre, Dr Goldsmith. I can't just put a play on because a man is poor. I hope I may still be counted your friend, sirs.

Johnson We never see you, Davy. You do not come into a room but you have an excuse to get out of it.

Garrick You may say so, sir, but I am kept out of your club.

Johnson I doubt your wife would give you permission to come.

Garrick I can only hope my absence has been of some comfort to you.

Johnson On the contrary. You are a lively fellow, Davy, the first in the world for sprightly conversation. I regret that our paths have crossed so infrequently of late, for you might help alleviate my melancholy. There is scarcely a day I do not rise with it in the morning and take it to bed at night. A dismal dread of death.

Garrick I am sorry to hear it.

Johnson It is a shame we cannot see eye to eye on Goldy's play. I should have liked for us to be reconciled and that might have been the means to do it. See, an invitation. You were to have joined us at our club next week.

Garrick But I have always been kept out.

Johnson We had no reason before, sir, but now we are furnished with one.

Goldsmith Perhaps I could read a little of my play? Kate disguised and Marlow. (*He reads.*) What a b–b–bawling in every p–part of the house, I have scarce a moment rep–pose. If I go to the b–b–best room –

Johnson We must read it, Goldy, or we will be here for eternity. (*Johnson reads.*) I go to the best room, there I find my host with his story. If I fly to the gallery, there we have my hostess with her curtsey down to the ground. I have at last got a moment to myself and now for recollection.

Garrick Did you call, sir? Did your honour call?

Johnson As for Miss Hardcastle, she's too grave and sentimental for me.

Garrick Did your honour call?

Johnson No, child. Besides, from the glimpse I had of her I think she squints.

Garrick I'm sure, sir, I heard the bell ring.

Johnson No, no. I have pleased my father, however, by coming down tomorrow I shall please myself by returning.

Garrick Perhaps the other gentlemen called, sir.

Johnson I tell you no.

Garrick I should be glad to know, sir; we have such a parcel of servants.

Johnson No, no, I tell you. Yes, child, I think I did call. I wanted . . . I wanted – I vow, child, you are vastly handsome.

Garrick Oh la, sir, you make one asham'd.

Johnson I never saw a more malicious eye. Yes, yes, my dear, I did call. Have you got any of your – a – what-do-you-call-it in the house?

Garrick No, sir, we have been out of that these ten days.

Johnson laughs.

Johnson You must not make me laugh, Davy, for I cannot continue if you do.

Garrick To see you laugh is a good thing, Doctor.

Goldsmith It puts one in mind of a great whale breaking water.

Johnson It is a creditable comedy, is it not, Davy?

Goldsmith (*to Garrick*) You would be fantastic in it.

Johnson The end of comedy is to make us merry.

Garrick May I take the invitation, sir?

Johnson gives it to him.

Goldsmith Does that mean you will do my p–play?

Johnson It is not fair to ask so direct, Goldy. Anyway, Davy must get his wife's permission.

Garrick No, sir, I make up my own mind. We may have had our differences but if *She Stoops to Conquer* continues to delight, you may be in luck, Dr Goldsmith.

Goldsmith (*gives a whoop*) I shall holla like a speaking trumpet!

Mrs Garrick Here, Doctor. A pudding. I supervised it myself.

Johnson A delectable meaty confection, ma'am. It shall glorify my table.

They exit. Mrs Garrick enters. She picks up play from table.

Mrs Garrick (*reads*) *She Stoops To Conquer or The Mistakes of a Night.* Did you tell them you had committed to Mr Cumberland's play?

Garrick suddenly folds up with pain.

(*sharply*) Davy!

He straightens up immediately.

Mrs Garrick You can't do them both.

Garrick No.

Mrs Garrick I'm sure you'll find a way to let the Doctor down gently.

SCENE THREE

Johnson Playreading: An attempt by the artistic management of a theatre to avoid the responsibility of office. A low word.

The actors. Garrick and Goldsmith.

Garrick (*concluding*) Tomorrow we shall gather all the poor of the parish about us, and the mistakes of the night shall be crown'd with a merry morning; so, boy, take her, and as you have been mistaken in the mistress, my wish is, that you may never be mistaken in the wife.

Actors politely applaud.

Goldsmith Thank you for your indulgence in allowing me not to read my p–p–play to you. Mr Garrick was uniformly excellent. Also I have to say the p–p–play is very good.

Garrick You are quite clear, Doctor, as to our purpose here today?

Goldsmith P–perfectly.

Garrick I am in the fortunate position of having to choose between two excellent plays. Reading each will assist me in my decision.

Goldsmith I'm sure you'll like mine the b–best.

Garrick Let me show you out, Doctor.

They exit.

Mrs Cibber Has he gone? I make the speech. Dear manager, dear, dear Garrick. And so on. Token of our esteem. Then we hand him the gloves. Who's got the gloves?

All You have.

Mrs Butler Nobody else got a look in.

Mrs Cibber And then he reads the card. Perhaps you would read it for now, Mr Cautherley.

Cautherley Shakespeare's gloves.

Macklin That's the twelfth pair I've seen.

Mrs Butler He had a lot of gloves.

Mrs Cibber Your voice has an excellent timbre, Mr Cautherley.

Mrs Barry Yes, it has.

Cautherley Thank you.

Macklin Playreading. What a time-wasting shenanigan. (*He pulls out bottle and swigs.*)

Mrs Cibber I was under the impression that you were no longer fond of alcohol, Mr Macklin.

Macklin You were ill informed, Mrs Cibber.

Mrs Butler In all honesty I should put that in the book, Mr Macklin.

Macklin Stuff the book.

Mrs Cibber I'm just a little concerned that if we persist in not hitting it off it will communicate itself in that subtle way it does to an audience. If you'd wash, it might help.

Macklin Lonely men don't wash.

Mrs Cibber That's why they're lonely. It's a vicious circle. Smelly: lonely – lonely: smelly.

Macklin I am astounded afresh by your ability to see nothing whatsoever, Mrs Cibber. Garrick knows full well which play he wants. This is a political exercise to appease the loser!

Cautherley Mr Garrick is an honourable man. I am sure he will choose the best play.

Macklin So, Mr Cautherley, you're an actor.

Cautherley Yes, sir, I hope to be.

Macklin Garrick has embraced you. You must have something.

Barry Yes, he has my parts. I am juve lead male and this is my wife. Mrs Barry and I are a package.

Mrs Barry Oh, I don't mind doing it with someone different for a change.

Barry Lavinia!

Mrs Barry Audiences don't like seeing husbands and wives play together. They know we only row really.

Barry No we don't!

Macklin (to Cautherley) So you are to follow in the master's footsteps?

Cautherley I hope to, sir.

Macklin The thing you ought to know, Mr Cautherley, is that once upon a time Garrick was the newest thing that had ever been seen. I'll give him that. But, and this is a little known fact, there was another before him and it was he who invented the whole new style. He who really fired the dart that fatally struck the past. And do you know who he was?

Cautherley No, sir.

Macklin No, nobody does, and that is why I like a drink.

Cautherley You mean it was you.

Macklin Sharp as a whistle, Mr Cautherley.

Mrs Butler 1737.

Macklin My Shylock.

Barry You can be sure, not a day goes past but we have his Shylock.

Macklin But rarely on stage, ma'am, that is the point.

Mrs Butler Anyway, the damp's got your gaberdine.

Barry Mr Garrick will not choose Dr Goldsmith's play, it is too low.

Cautherley Low?

Barry It mocks gentility. All the characters live in the country.

Mrs Barry Someone has to live in the country, Mr Barry, else we'd never get any eggs.

Barry There must be other ways of getting eggs, Lavinia.

Macklin No, they must always come out of a chicken's arse.

Cautherley I often find plays rather tedious but I enjoyed this one.

Mrs Cibber I have similar concerns to Mr Barry. I prefer to play characters of spotless virtue, Mr Cautherley, and in this way I avoid drawing attention to my unusual domestic arrangements.

Mrs Butler Her first husband was a bastard who sold her to a gentleman for a night who then fell in love with her and her first husband wouldn't leave her so now she has two.

Mrs Cibber Thank you, Mrs Butler. It was my misfortune to have two husbands. I don't recommend it, Mr

Cautherley, because of the irreparable damage to one's reputation and the extra laundry. Mrs Hardcastle falls in the pond and she has been given to me.

Mrs Barry I'm sure I would do either play, although Kate Hardcastle does get to kiss.

Barry Kate Hardcastle is a trollop.

Mrs Barry Can't you stick to your own part?

Mrs Butler Now you are poor second to Mr Cautherley, that's Lumpkin.

Cautherley Lumpkin is a mischief-maker but it's hard not to like him.

Barry That's not the sort of thing a gentleman would enjoy playing. But perhaps you're not a gentleman, sir.

Mrs Cibber Mr Barry!

Barry I only know that he has come and taken my parts!

Cautherley I am quite content to give an account of myself, sir.

Mrs Cibber That will not be necessary.

Cautherley I was found on the steps of this theatre.

Pause.

With a note pinned to me reading 'Gentleman'.

Barry I could pin a note to myself saying 'King of Sweden'.

Macklin Try actor first, sir.

Barry Ditto, sir.

Macklin Pup!

Mrs Butler Where's your company spirit, Mr Macklin?

Macklin In my bottle. (*Macklin advances.*)

Barry Stop him, Mrs Butler. He'll soon be in a state of advanced inebriation.

Mrs Barry Run, darling!

Mrs Butler Mr Macklin! This is definitely going in the book!

> *A general tussle to remove Macklin from Barry. Enter Garrick and Cumberland.*

Mrs Butler Mr Garrick.

> *Actors part.*

Garrick May I introduce you to the Reverend Richard Cumberland? The author of *The Fashionable Lover.*

> *Cumberland surveys the unseemly spectacle.*

Cumberland Hello.

All Hello.

Cumberland Would you like me to describe the fountain of my inspiration?

Garrick Better not. Let's start. (*He signals to each actor in turn.*) Mrs Barry would play Augusta Aubrey. A young beautiful orphan. Mrs Cibber, Mrs Macintosh. A bitter, fading middle-aged woman of thirty-five or so.

Macklin No acting necessary.

Garrick Mr Macklin, Hamish Macleod. A Scottish gentleman. Mr Cautherley, Charles Millwood. A good young gentleman. Mr Barry, Lord Aberville. A rake who reforms. I should play Uncle Mortimer. A benign soul.

Mrs Cibber It seems a very uplifting sort of play with such a lot of good gentlemen in it. I appear to be the only unreformed character.

Cumberland And you are not on long.

Mrs Cibber Ah . . .

Garrick Reverend Cumberland has kindly agreed to give us a brief résumé of his play before he reads it.

Cumberland The hero, Charles Millwood, returns to London from his plantation on the Island of Tobago. He is a good-natured young gentleman and in the bustle of the dockside he inadvertently sets about one of the porters with his cane. Not used to such treatment the fellow pushes Charles into the water. He is pulled . . .

  A buzzing sound (Macklin).

Garrick Let me explain, Mr Cumberland. We have developed a system over time where, if an actor feels there is a point to be raised during a reading, they make a small noise to alert the company's attention to the problem. I feel it is too early in the process for that, Macklin.

Macklin I was merely going to enquire whether Charles loses any clothes during his mishap?

Cumberland Ah, I hadn't thought.

Macklin For example, if he lost his breeches we could be in a very sensitive situation.

Garrick No one is suggesting for a moment that he loses his breeches.

Macklin Because you can't have an arse on stage, Mr Garrick.

Garrick No, but I have often been blessed with them in my company.

Mrs Cibber In any case he may have been wearing a long shirt.

Garrick These are small details. Mrs Butler can see to them later.

Mrs Butler Oh yes, I'm a magician.

Cumberland Charles soon discovers the terrible truth of the loss of his papers from his breeches pocket. He breaks down in tears. The papers had been proof that Augusta Aubrey, the young woman he had never seen but had fallen in love with by correspondence, was really a wealthy heiress. Charles's Uncle Mortimer had always refused permission for him to marry Augusta because she was poor, and she submitted.

Buzz (Mrs Barry).

Mrs Barry Why would she do that?

Garrick Because she is essentially good, Mrs Barry.

Barry That will take a deal of explaining to you, so I suggest we avoid it at present.

Mrs Barry Apologise, Mr Barry.

Barry When you apologise to me for your behaviour last night.

Mrs Barry Your second entrance was entirely designed to upstage me.

Barry I was trying to refocus the performance.

Mrs Butler It's all in the book, Mr Garrick.

Barry She was too busy curtseying to some oaf in a box.

Mrs Barry It's my right to make new friends.

Macklin She's got a lot of them out there, Mr Barry.

Barry You were practically falling out of your dress.

Mrs Barry storms out.

Lavinia!

Pause.

37

Garrick Please continue, Reverend.

Cumberland Hurrying to his uncle's house, Charles comes across the path of the most beautiful woman he has ever seen, whom he desires to –

Buzz (Macklin).

– get to know better.

Garrick Mr Macklin.

Macklin Sorry, Mr Garrick.

Cumberland Unknown to him, she and his cousin Augusta are one and the same person.

Mrs Butler I knew that.

Cumberland Now he is on the horns of a dilemma. Should he tell his uncle the truth about the papers he had concealed about his private . . .

Buzz.

. . . down his trousers . . .

Buzz.

Garrick Can we restrain ourselves?

Cumberland . . . in his pocket. Or should he forget them and be free to propose to the unknown woman he wishes to . . .

Buzz.

Marry.

Garrick Mr Macklin.

Cumberland These constant interruptions, Mr Garrick.

Garrick I do apologise.

Cumberland You don't get them in church.

Mrs Cibber (*refers to Macklin*) He has been drinking.

Garrick Just put a cork in it, Macklin.

Cumberland Mr Garrick, I wish to withdraw my play.

Garrick From Drury Lane?

Cumberland No, from the actors. I feel you alone are the person qualified to make a decision on the future of my work. I wish to cast no aspersions on the present company, but actors are generally a pleasanter experience when viewed from a distance. Good day. (*He exits.*)

Macklin And bog off.

Garrick in some physical discomfort.

Garrick (*to the company*) I have always considered actors troublesome creatures and today you have gone further, if that is possible, in consolidating that opinion. Good day. Mr Macklin, I shall be reconsidering my appearance in your benefit.

Mrs Butler Never mind, Mr Garrick. No real harm done. You won't have to pay the actors for the afternoon.

Garrick Yes. Thank you, Mrs Butler.

Mrs Butler ushers out actors.

Cautherley I'm sorry, Mr Garrick. But it did seem an unlikely play.

Cautherley exits, Mrs Garrick enters.

Garrick Don't say anything.

Mrs Garrick I'm not saying anything.

Pause.

But now you're in the same position only worse. Dr Goldsmith's hopes are raised and you have offended

Mr Cumberland. Lady Kingston has sent over a large cheese and a crate of claret. Do I have to send it back?

Garrick Dr Goldsmith has influential friends of a different sort.

Mrs Garrick It's the great roles people want to see. You should be saving your strength for them. And the good thing about Shakespeare is he's dead, we don't have to pay him.

Garrick You have a new play in the repertoire otherwise writers attack you! Shakespeare was a new writer once.

Mrs Garrick Of course. But you must think practically. Dr Goldsmith's play is low. You don't want to be selling the patent for a theatre that has been torn apart by riots.

Garrick Goldsmith is a man of some genius.

Mrs Garrick Not as a playwright, looking at his last effort.

Garrick This one seems rather better than Cumberland's play.

Mrs Garrick But people like his sort of thing.

Garrick They did . . . the fashion for sentiment seems to be cooling a little. That's the trouble with getting older – you get less decisive.

Mrs Garrick Mr Garrick. The brochures are printed on Tuesday.

She exits. Mrs Butler crosses the stage.

Mrs Butler Special delivery, Mr Garrick. Three tubs of French polish.

Hannah More enters.

Hannah Mr Garrick. We've met before. I was fourteen. I'd been taken to see *Hamlet*. I fainted. I was carried into your office. You were kind enough to enquire after me.

Garrick Ah . . . No French polish. I've never heard that one before. My dear young lady . . .

Hannah Then I read in a newspaper that this was rumoured to be your last season. And I had to come and tell you.

Garrick Tell me?

Hannah Of my extreme admiration. I am a writer.

Garrick Of plays?

She takes out a small leather bookmark.

Hannah Yes.

Garrick I'm not in a position to put on your play, madam, I won't even read it.

Hannah Mr Garrick . . .

Garrick I may never read another play as long as I live. Good day.

Hannah You mistake me, I would never try to influence a decision of yours. You are a great artist and the greatest man I've ever met. May I ask you to sign my bookmark, which I shall treasure with all my heart?

Garrick Very well. (*He signs it.*)

Hannah I have watched you many times and been moved to emotions I have never experienced.

Garrick But you know you must make an appointment next time.

Hannah This will be the brightest day of my life.

Garrick Oh dear. Have you come far?

Hannah Harrow. I walked. I couldn't afford a coach. I'm a schoolteacher. Today I claimed a cough and set off.

He gives her the bookmark.

Thank you. Your eyes, Mr Garrick, are the most piercing I have ever seen. And the kindest and most intelligent. And the most beautiful, I think.

Garrick Well, they are two balls side by side. So do you come to the theatre often?

Hannah I spend half my wages. I don't eat breakfasts. I have seen you play every part in your repertoire. I enjoyed you in Mr Kelly's *False Delicacy* and also *The Foundling* and *Wonder of Wonders*. But Lear is your greatest.

Garrick You seem very passionate about the theatre. Miss . . .?

Hannah More.

Garrick Perhaps if you leave your play with me, I may offer you some advice.

She gets to her knees.

Hannah I'm overcome with gratitude, dear Mr Garrick.

Garrick What are you doing?

Hannah Kneeling.

Garrick My dear young lady.

Hannah Because to me everything that is beautiful in the world is before me now.

Garrick I repeat, I cannot offer you a production.

Hannah Just to breathe the same air.

Mrs Garrick comes out of secret panel.

Garrick This is my wife, Eva. Eva, Miss More.

Mrs Garrick We can always do with help. How are you with stuffing, Miss More?

SCENE FOUR: ROMANTIC COMEDY

Hannah alone in Garrick's office, tidying up files.
Cautherley enters. Hannah looks up.

Hannah Can I help you?

Cautherley I came to see Mr Garrick.

Hannah Do take a seat.

Cautherley Will he be long?

Hannah I should expect so. There's a considerable
amount of organising to do. Mr Garrick keeps everything.
A copy of all his correspondence, of which he receives
copious amounts. I hope you don't mind if I carry on.
(*She continues to sort his files.*) Perhaps there's something
I can help you with, Mr . . .?

Cautherley Cautherley. No, no. It was Mr Garrick
I particularly wanted to see.

She regards him.

It's about a part, Miss . . .?

Hannah More. I am a writer. My best-known work is
The Trials of Percy.

Cautherley Percy who?

Hannah Lord Percy.

Cautherley It sounds good.

Pause.

This part. I hope to persuade Mr Garrick to let me play
it. I think I'd be rather good.

Hannah That's for others to say, I suspect.

Cautherley I don't mean to sound boastful. I'm just rather relieved. I owe Mr Garrick a great debt. I am his protégé.

Hannah You are?

Cautherley Yes. Mr Garrick has always looked after me.

Hannah You are very fortunate, Mr Cautherley, to have had Mr Garrick as a guardian. I was under the guardianship of teachers of religious instruction.

Cautherley You seem to have turned out all right.

Hannah What do you mean?

Cautherley You seem to have turned out . . . nice.

   Beat.

Hannah Oh. Here's a letter you sent. (*She reads.*) Dear Mr Garrick. School is dull. I am not very happy. You've spelt it 'hoppy'.

Cautherley I'm not a good speller.

Hannah I was reading at the age of two. (*reading on*) One boy at school his name is Jeffries; I am to clean his shoes every morning before breakfast because his father is Lord Jeffries. Love, Sam. I don't read them as a rule. Mr Garrick is very exercised about which play he should put on. Which play do you prefer, Mr Cautherley?

Cautherley Dr Goldsmith's. It is a play in very good spirits.

Hannah To you, perhaps. But for middling people like myself it offends deeply. Mischief is rewarded and deception goes unpunished.

Cautherley But it's funny.

Hannah That is not a sufficient argument that justifies cruel and selfish behaviour. I'm sure Mr Garrick will refuse it.

Cautherley Mr Garrick used to say comedy is a spirit. Have you ever been for a walk in the countryside, Miss More?

Hannah Alone, Mr Cautherley?

Cautherley Perfectly alone.

Hannah Only once and I shouldn't have.

Cautherley Well, imagine that you're there now. It's a sunny day and suddenly you step off the path and find yourself in the shade of a wood. All the sounds are different. And you stop and you stare at a tangle of dark leaves and you can't be sure there isn't something there and it's not a bird and it's not a dog but you're sure there is something and the thought pleases you and it sends a shudder down your back. It's something old, something that won't do as you bid it. And do you know what it's doing?

Hannah No.

Cautherley It's laughing at the fool you're making of yourself staring at the bush.

Hannah slaps him.

Cautherley That's the spirit of comedy. It always tricks people into revealing themselves.

Hannah I'm sorry, Mr Cautherley, I shouldn't have struck you.

She kisses him. Garrick enters.

Hannah Your handwriting is very French, Mr Garrick.

Garrick Is it?

Hannah It has a natural curling elegance. (*She exits.*)

Cautherley I was wondering if I could have a word, sir.

Garrick Certainly, Sam.

Cautherley Mr Garrick, I've fallen in love.

Garrick Aaah . . .

Cautherley With a part. I wasn't sure I was an actor, sir, but this is a good sign, I think.

Garrick Mr Millwood is a very handsome gentleman with an elegant turn of phrase.

Cautherley Hastings in his way is appealing, too.

Garrick So you wish to play Mr Hastings. You have a feeling for him, you've taken to the part? My question is, should I risk affronting my audience by going for *She Stoops*? Because audiences are not tame. They're not averse to throwing things. They once threw a man from the gallery to the pit.

Cautherley But I don't want to play Mr Hastings. I want to play Tony Lumpkin.

Garrick Lumpkin! But you are a natural Hastings, Sam. A young gentleman.

Cautherley But the actor who plays Lumpkin, sir, will have a lot of fun. He's always drinking and singing down the Three Pigeons. You were on the verge of indulging me. I very much hope, sir, you will.

Garrick Lumpkin is a different matter altogether, sir.

Cautherley You once played such parts, sir.

Garrick Not any more, Sam.

Cautherley Father-in-law has been calling me a whelp, and hound this half year. Now if I pleased I could be so revenged upon the old grumbletonian. But then I'm afraid – afraid of what? I shall soon be worth fifteen hundred a year, and let him frighten me out of that if he can.

Garrick Good, Sam. Yes. Yes. You've caught the spirit of it.

Mrs Garrick enters.

Sam was just expressing a preference for a certain part, Mrs Garrick.

Mrs Garrick So I heard. Actors can't choose their parts, Sam – if they did there'd be no one to play the messengers.

Garrick He has instinct.

Mrs Garrick Sam?

Garrick I had that. It makes all the difference . . .

Mrs Garrick I was an artist too, Sam, a dancer in the best theatres in Europe. It wouldn't have been proper for me to continue when I married Mr Garrick. There are considerations other than instinct. A dog has instinct.

Garrick Sam, would you mind?

Cautherley Mr Garrick, Mrs Garrick.

Sam exits.

Mrs Garrick Reverend Cumberland's play has no hint of impropriety.

Garrick He wouldn't know impropriety if it crawled up his cassock.

Mrs Garrick You can laugh, Mr Garrick, but you know how cruel scandal can be. People in scandals lose everything.

Garrick There's not going to be a scandal!

Mrs Garrick Good, because we'll retire soon. Then what would we do with ourselves?

Garrick Retired people get busier.

Mrs Garrick Not if they're being ignored. We'd just be staring at each other over the dining-room table. There were rumours when we married.

Garrick Actresses get pregnant because they're like that. Management cannot be held responsible.

Mrs Garrick Whether it's true or not, people like to believe the worst. Sam's first part. Your protégé. Do you want people to take him for a Lumpkin? Don't throw it all away in the end. Your reputation. Everything you deserve.

She exits. Contemplatively: Garrick goes over to a skip and pulls out a tobacconist's apron. He puts it on. He dresses himself as Abel Drugger.

SCENE FIVE

The rest of the company gathers. The cast of The Alchemist.

Macklin Where is Garrick?

Garrick Here, sir.

Macklin You have been with us . . .

Garrick Three days.

Macklin You are determined to follow the course upon which you have set yourself?

Garrick Yes, sir. But if I may be allowed to explain once more, Mr Macklin.

Macklin That will not be necessary.

Cross I have not had instructions from Mr Fleetwood . . .

Macklin I am manager in the absence of Fleetwood, Mr Cross. Where is Bounce?

Bounce Here, sir. Cedric Bounce. Low comedian. I was always Mr Drugger till this date, sir. But I am shifted about, sir, at Mr Garrick's convenience. He wished Mr Drugger.

Young Barry It is a low part.

O'Ryan Low indeed.

Bounce I specialise in those. My pratfalls are a joy. I inherited my father's extra-large shoes, sir, which till this day I was accustomed to wear on the wrong feet whilst playing Drugger.

Mrs Butler Shame.

Young Barry It is a shame.

Mrs Butler You see, even Master Barry thinks so.

Young Barry I am playing Kastril, the angry boy. And I am angry.

Bounce What appliances do you favour, Mr Garrick? Buttock extensions or the comedy nose?

Garrick I favour nothing of the sort.

Bounce Nothing?

O'Ryan Nothing?

Flint It is the worst thing I ever saw.

Macklin We are in agreement with Mrs Flint. This is the matter, sir, we wish to call to your attention, sir.

Mrs Butler You have to make them laugh, otherwise they want their money back.

Woffington Mr Garrick is too tragic an actor to consider anything as unworthy as a laugh.

Macklin He prefers a good death so he can wring every last drop of sympathy from the punters and leaving nothing for the poor bastards who come on after him. Show him your Drugger, Mr Bounce.

O'Ryan Oblige us, sir.

Bounce Surely, I pull a long face so. Hanging lip, you see. With my hair disarranged I look a regular booby. I come in. I fall over. I shake hands with the fire irons.

Mrs Butler Oh, it is priceless.

Macklin How shall you do it, Garrick?

Garrick I shall do as it says in the script: 'Enter'.

Macklin You must not let us down, Garrick.

Flint Coins.

Macklin If a play is shouted off, we actors are out of pocket.

Garrick Nowhere in the play does Mr Jonson indicate that Mr Drugger is a cretin. He is a tobacconist and that is how I shall play him.

Bounce It'll never work, Mr Garrick.

Mrs Butler I won't be able to look.

Barry I will look, for it is a very bad thing to take another man's part.

Macklin Mr Garrick, sir, remove your apron.

Cross I must protest, Mr Macklin.

Macklin I elect Mr Bounce to be Mr Drugger.

Garrick My name is on the flyers.

Mrs Butler He once killed a man in a mix-up over a wig.

O'Ryan Straight through the eye with a stick.

Macklin I am not to be lightly crossed.

Garrick It is curtain up in five minutes, Mr Macklin, and I shall be making an entrance.

Macklin Very well. We shall have to use force.

Flint Hit him!

Garrick I am ready for you.

Cross Mr Macklin, this is highly irregular.

Macklin Stick to writing your show reports, Mr Cross. Mrs Woffington.

Mrs Woffington takes out a pistol. Uproar from company.

Garrick Good Lord.

O'Ryan Shit.

Mrs Cibber Stop this!

Flint Shoot him!

Macklin Play Drugger in the time-honoured way or Mr Bounce takes your place.

Garrick I will be playing Mr Drugger.

Macklin Very well. Bounce, where is your nose?

Bounce Here, Mr Macklin.

Macklin (*to Garrick*) Mr Garrick requires it.

Gives it to Garrick, who puts it on.

Macklin And the shoes.

Mrs Butler That's better.

O'Ryan That's funny.

These are produced and put on. General laughter.

Macklin Excellent.

Flint Like Bounce. Good.

Garrick gives a big sigh.

Young Barry What's wrong with him?

Garrick sighs again.

He doesn't like his shoes. Is that it?

Garrick shrugs his shoulders.

Maybe his nose pinches?

O'Ryan He's dejected.

Macklin He's acting.

Mrs Cibber Address him as Mr Drugger and perhaps he will answer.

Mrs Butler Go on, Master Barry.

Young Barry Are you Mr Drugger? The tobacconist?

Bounce He is not Abel Drugger. For Abel is a laugh a minute.

Garrick I have a little shop.

Mrs Butler That will be the tobacco shop.

Mrs Cibber They say Garrick becomes the part he plays. As if he's possessed.

Young Barry Shall we stick him with a pin?

Cross Leave him, Master Barry.

Garrick I sell pins.

O'Ryan Pins.

Garrick I go to see a man about my shop. I am an honest working man. I am not the quickest man in my street but I am honest and straightforward. Perhaps people will hoodwink me, but so be it. I live by principles and also by tobacco.

Macklin Enough of this.

Garrick I seek to know, sir, by alchemy, where to put my shelves and my boxes. And also my pots.

Flint It's not right.

Woffington We know you are an actor, sir, and so are we.

Garrick Very well. Must I go forth with these things on me?

Macklin You must.

Mrs Butler Oh dear. They don't look funny any more. They look sad.

Barry I think I may burst into tears.

Bounce They was always funny on me.

Mrs Butler That is because you are an idiot.

Cross Two minutes to curtain.

Garrick takes off the nose.

Macklin The nose, Mr Garrick.

Pause. Garrick does nothing. Woffington drops pistol.

Woffington Let him go on.

Macklin And ruin a good night's takings? Drugger is a great favourite.

Woffington Let him make a fool of himself and then he can disappear.

Garrick Mr Macklin, for two years I have watched your every performance. I've learnt everything from you. You are sublime in your naturalness. You have affected a revolution!

Macklin That's true.

Garrick Your Shylock was a human being and not a comic turn.

Macklin But Drugger is a low character.

Garrick He is a working man, but we may still have sympathy with him.

Cross Curtain up.

Macklin What do you say, Mrs Woffington?

Woffington Working people work. Nothing would get done if they were as simple as they're made out.

Mrs Butler That's right, Mr Macklin.

Macklin Well, well, perhaps we'll see how Mr Garrick does. Now you mustn't mind me, I've a temper that flares up upon occasion, that's all.

Cross Mr Garrick. The Prologue.

Garrick Thank you.

As he goes to exit, Mrs Woffington catches him.

Woffington My Rosalind was sublime in its naturalness, wanker.

Garrick Mrs Woffington. The flowers. I send them. (*He exits.*)

Bounce Nothing beats a buttock extension.

The rest listen. We hear Garrick faintly speak the Prologue.

Garrick
 I stand before you, men and women of the town . . .

Cross You'll bounce back, Mr Bounce.

Bounce What do you think, Mr Macklin?

Macklin does not answer. Bounce picks up comedy accoutrements and starts to go.

Mrs Butler Where are you going?

Bounce I've got an uncle in Yorkshire.

SCENE SIX: POLITICAL THEATRE

Present: Mrs Cibber, Mrs Butler, Mrs Woffington, Betty Flint, Garrick, Macklin, Cross, Master Barry, Bounce, Mr O'Ryan.

Cross I call this meeting of the Drury Lane company to order. Speaker the first.

Mrs Butler Mrs Butler, dresser. I have begged Mr Fleetwood on my own behalf and that of my poor children that he should pay what he owes me but he always looks at me sadly and says it cannot be done. This has now continued for six months and if it had not been for the generosity of the actors I am sure we would all be dead. And although Mr Fleetwood says he is an honest man he is not starving as we are. I am now frightened to leave my house as it is put about that I am to be arrested for debt and thrown into a sponging house and then my poor children will starve for sure.

O'Ryan Theophilus O'Ryan, supporting actor. That is because he is a gambler.

Macklin Charles Macklin, actor. You can't hold it against a man that he gambles.

Mrs Butler Point of information. Charles Macklin and Mr Fleetwood are old friends.

Macklin Point of information. Not any more.

Mrs Butler I have nothing against gambling *per se*, but I do when it's with our wages.

All Agreed.

Flint Betty Flint, candle-tender. Newgate.

Mrs Butler The candle-tenders are in the same boat as the dressers. Some are thrown into Newgate for non-payment of debt and the rest will soon follow.

Flint Bill Williams.

Mrs Butler And Mr Bill Williams, prop-maker, has died of want, God rest his soul.

All Amen.

Flint Food.

Mrs Butler Betty Flint reminds us there was no one that made wooden food as good as he did. Mr Cross, the prompter has seen no wages since . . .

Cross Easter. But that is the business we are in, Mrs Butler.

Mrs Butler It is a bad business that will not pay its workers, Mr Cross.

Cross If it were not Mr Fleetwood, it would be someone worse.

O'Ryan Theophilus O'Ryan, supporting actor. I have personally applied to Mr Fleetwood on my own behalf and that of us all several times in recent weeks. Those being when his whereabouts were known.

Macklin His whereabouts are the Fox and Grapes on Argyll Street.

Mrs Butler Point of information. He is a bastard. I would go down to the Fox and Grapes only I don't trust myself not to beat him about the head with one of Mr Williams's wooden foodstuffs. Then my poor children would have the ignominy of seeing their mother transported. My question is this: will the actors withdraw their labour until the money that is owed us all is paid?

Macklin Charles Macklin, actor. What if we lose our jobs? Fleetwood can be a right petty bastard.

Uproar from company.

Macklin What do you say, Garrick?

Garrick David Garrick, actor. I'm just listening, Mr Macklin. I've been with you barely a year.

Macklin You are our leading actor now, Garrick. We invite your response.

Garrick David Garrick, actor. It seems extraordinary that Mr Fleetwood should choose to treat our distinguished company in so cavalier a manner. Does he need to be reminded that he has some of the finest players in the country? Mr Macklin here began a revolution with his reinterpretation of Shylock that sent shock-waves across Europe. I have followed in his footsteps.

Mrs Butler We all enjoyed your Abel Drugger, Mr Garrick, and I for one said so at the time.

O'Ryan Mr Fleetwood cares nothing for the theatre. He throws away the money he should be spending on new costumes and scenery at the gaming table. No wonder our audiences desert us for Covent Garden.

Mrs Butler He is then forced to cut us to half-pay –

Bounce / Flint No pay, no pay.

Mrs Butler – and then to no pay whatsoever. We must demand what is owed us.

Garrick David Garrick, actor. We can do more. We can demand our own licence to play. When we have our own theatre we can pay ourselves and choose the plays we perform. When we do good work, people will respect us.

Some Hear, hear!

Woffington Peg Woffington, actor. There are only two licences and they have already been given!

Garrick The Lord Chamberlain will be told of Fleetwood's desertion. He will then grant a third.

Woffington The point of a licence is to limit the performance of plays to two theatres only. The government of this country is nervous of plays, which is why it introduced the principle of a licence in the first place. The law will not be changed on our account.

Garrick My dear Mrs Woffington, we have the moral imperative.

Woffington Point of information. David Garrick thinks he is in a play.

Mrs Butler Point of information. They're having a row.

Mrs Cibber It is strange to think that anyone would be scared of a play.

Cross Madam, please address yourself to the meeting in the correct manner.

Mrs Cibber Mrs Cibber, first singer. Sorry.

Master Barry Master Barry, child actor. And we must always be playing in pantomime 'cause it brings in the punters and I don't like the dogs in them for one bit me on the arm.

Bounce Bounce, low comedian that was. Presently stage-hand. Mr Garrick has only been in the business two minutes. What does he know?

Garrick We are in an intolerable situation. I know that, Mr Bounce.

Woffington It could be worse if we have to crawl back to Fleetwood.

Garrick Audiences don't come to see Fleetwood. I propose we refuse to play until we are granted our own theatre.

Woffington I say we should apply again to Mr Fleetwood.

Mrs Butler Point of information. Mrs Woffington and Mr Fleetwood are very close. I'm not saying any more.

Woffington That's my business and nothing to do with this business.

Garrick David Garrick, actor. We must all hope that Mrs Woffington will not let her personal interests prejudice her to the common good.

Mrs Cibber Mrs Cibber, first singer. It is indeed an honour, Mr Garrick, to hear our beleaguered profession dignified by your stirring rhetoric.

O'Ryan Theophilus O'Ryan, supporting actor, specialising in supporting parts. I support Mr Garrick.

Woffington No wonder you put audiences to sleep, Mr O'Ryan.

O'Ryan No need to get personal, Mrs Woffington.

Cross Let us take it to the vote. Mr Garrick proposes we withdraw our labour until such time as a licence for an actors' theatre is granted us.

Macklin Charles Macklin, actor and revolutionary interpreter of Shylock. We did not trust Mr Garrick when he first came. To our shame we threatened him. I stood in his way then, but as his merit upon the stage is vastly superior to mine I will not stand in it now. I vote with Garrick.

Cross All in favour say 'aye'.

All (*except Woffington, Cross, Bounce*) Aye.

Cross Against.

Woffington/Cross/Bounce Nay.

Cross The motion is carried.

Macklin
Let no man break his word.
If every ducat in six thousand ducats
Were in six parts and every part a ducat
I would not draw them – I would have my bond.

*Actors disperse, shaking hands, etc. Garrick keeps
back Woffington.*

Garrick We could do with a capital actress on our side.

Woffington I am on your side, Davy. I just think you're
wasting your time.

Garrick Can't I persuade you?

Woffington They won't give actors a theatre.

Garrick I happen to have a personal letter from the Lord
Chamberlain praising my Richard.

Woffington I have plenty of letters myself. I don't hold
anything by them. You are funny, Mr Garrick. As if
what we want ever matters to anything. Actors must be
charming and win favour that way.

Garrick Can I see you later?

Woffington I might be able to fit you in.

Mrs Cibber approaches.

Mrs Cibber Mr Garrick!

Woffington walks off.

I was wondering if I might have a word with you. Time will sit very heavily upon me now there is no theatre to come to.

Garrick We'll have our own theatre soon.

Mrs Cibber No one talks to me outside the theatre. I'm a disgrace. I will meet no one except my two husbands. Perhaps I may be forced to drown myself!

Garrick It should only be a matter of weeks, Mrs Cibber. Surely you can avoid ponds in the meantime.

Mrs Cibber And I won't see you any more, Mr Garrick.

Garrick Well, I shall be around and about.

Mrs Cibber That's what I thought, and I thought that if you had some spare time, you might consider giving me some advice on acting. I would be very grateful. I do have rooms in town. If you're passing, I should be glad to see you. (*She hands him a key.*) That might make the whole situation quite bearable.

She exits. Garrick follows Woffington.

SCENE SEVEN

Night. A room. It soon becomes clear that someone is being amorous. Grunts, etc. Someone gets up.

Duke Thanks.

He stumbles out. Garrick gets out from under bed.

Garrick Never again. Why should I cower under the furniture?

Woffington Because you're an actor and he's the Duke of Kingston.

Garrick We wouldn't be in this situation if you could restrict the number of your gentlemen callers.

Woffington He pays for the room.

Garrick Our room!

Woffington It's my room.

Garrick I want us to live like a normal, respectable couple with a plaque outside our front door saying, 'Mr Garrick and Mrs Woffington'. It should be like saying 'solicitors' or 'dentists'. It shouldn't be an invitation for every randy aristocrat to pop up for a free shag.

Woffington The theatre is an unreliable source of income.

Garrick I tried to change that, but you wouldn't come in with us.

Woffington It's a good thing I didn't. Look where it got Mr Macklin.

Garrick Everybody blames me, don't they?

Woffington Well, Macklin blames you. But then he lost his job.

Garrick If actors were respectable, people might have listened to us.

Woffington He'll be back in a minute.

Garrick Will he?

Woffington For his gloves. You can tell him what you think then.

Garrick Perhaps I will.

Woffington You're all talk. You'll be diving under the bed the minute he walks through the door.

Duke calls off, 'Woff.'

Garrick I can't stand the noises he makes.

Woffington Get under the bed.

Garrick I'm grateful for your concern, madam.

Woffington Go on!

Enter Duke. Garrick dives under the bed.

Duke I forgot my gloves. Why don't you beat me for being a bad boy?

Woffington That's what you deserve. A great kick.

Duke I like the sound of that. Will you do it, Woff?

Woffington I'm sorely tempted.

Duke That's what I love about you, Woff: you're fiery. I look in your eyes and I see fire, fire, fire. Burn me. Drip wax on my tenderest places.

Woffington I'll get a candle.

Garrick crawls out from under the bed.

Garrick Here. (*He holds out a stump of candle.*) It was sticking in my back.

Duke Who's this?

Garrick My name is Garrick.

Duke Garrick?

Garrick The actor.

Duke What were you doing under our bed?

Garrick I was hiding, sir.

Duke Were you?

Garrick And then I decided it was behaviour ill becoming a gentleman.

Duke But not an actor.

Garrick The two are indistinguishable in my book. I have decided to give Mrs Woffington here an ultimatum. She must choose between the two of us.

Woffington What?

Duke How dare you come into my bed, actor?

Woffington It's my bed.

Duke Placing your stinking carcass between my sheets.

Woffington They're my sheets.

Duke Waving your stinking pizzle at my whore!

Woffington Oh, for God's sake!

Duke hits Garrick round the face.

Duke You putrid actor.

Garrick I own that is my profession.

Duke I may have to shoot you. Apologise.

Garrick What for?

Duke For being an actor, actor.

Woffington He stays here sometimes.

Duke In my room.

Woffington It's my room.

Duke I think you'll find I own the street. I'm giving you an ultimatum, Mrs Woffington. Get rid of him and the others and I'll sign you over five hundred pounds per annum. For life.

Woffington For life?

He turns to Garrick.

Duke Richard the Third, wasn't it?

Garrick Yes.

Duke You have apparently abandoned the rhythmic incantations and soporific rocking motions of your predecessors.

Garrick I have.

Duke Isn't it arrogance to presume that you can transcend a tradition that has served the public for centuries?

Garrick It seemed to me to be the right thing.

Duke I saw your Richard. You certainly execute the passions most poignantly and easily.

Garrick My journey to this point has not been an easy one, Your Grace. I was born in Birmingham.

Duke Definingly unpropitious.

Garrick Of a large and impecunious family. My dad was garrisoned in Malta and always forgot to write. I used to stand on the table and clown about to try to cheer Mum up.

Duke A charming picture.

Garrick I was hoping it might persuade you not to shoot me.

Duke Oh that. (*He puts gun away.*) I am only sorry that we had to become acquainted in such circumstances. I am a great theatre-lover and can only consider it a sadness I could not be of service to you in what might have been a most illustrious career.

Woffington Look at you, chatting away. You'd think you'd known each other for years, when the truth is you've both been fucking the same woman.

Duke It does happen. I shall see you at the theatre tomorrow.

Woffington You will not. Because I choose Garrick.

Duke I shall retire for the time being and let the heat out of the moment. I leave you with this thought, Mr Garrick: what's the point of being the greatest actor of your generation if you don't survive to prove it?

Interval.

A BALLETIC INTERLUDE

Voice Madam Violetta. The Austrian Violet.

Mrs Garrick appears dressed in violet and partly as a violet. She performs a short burst of eighteenth-century ballet. Applause as she finishes.

Mrs Garrick Thank you, everybody. I am very happy in your country. Everything here is very pleasant. I am most happy to the Duke and Duchess for taking care of me. I shall be available for social engagements. On my first time of dancing in England I wear long knickers, but I quickly see that this is not the fashion and now I wear short knickers. Thank you.

Act Two

Garrick's office.

Johnson To enlighten. To illuminate. To supply with
light, to instruct, to furnish with increase of knowledge,
to cheer, to exhilarate, to gladden, to supply with sight,
to quicken in the faculty of vision.

Garrick Have a look at this. (*Picks up a retractable
knife. Stabs himself.*) Marvellous, isn't it?

Johnson In the sense of a thing beyond belief, Davy,
certainly.

Garrick How is work on the dictionary going?

Johnson Tardily, protractedly, in a snail-like fashion.

Garrick I'm sorry to hear it. May I enquire about the
Prologue?

Johnson You may, sir.

Garrick Do you have it, sir?

Johnson I do have it. For I possess it, sir. I entertain it,
I have grasped the meaning and point of it. I have
suffered it, endured it, given birth to it, created it, in
short I own it and am now conveying it to you, sir.

Garrick May I see it?

Johnson No, sir, you may not. For it is in my head.

Garrick I long to hear it. I'm speaking it tonight at the
opening.

67

Johnson Indeed, sir, I hope you are, for that was the purpose in my composing it. The meat of it, sir, is thus: that a new era is dawning for the stage over which you will preside.

Garrick That's very good.

Johnson That is nothing, sir. For had you heard the pungent and rigorous versification in which I have crafted the sentiments, you could then claim satisfaction.

Garrick I await it, sir!

Pause.

Johnson Ah.

Garrick Yes?

Johnson I have it not, sir. As in one that lacks possessions. I have had it all and now no longer.

Garrick Does that mean you have forgotten it, sir?

Johnson Forgotten, sir, as we must all be. Neglected, put away, immured, sir, in the grave.

Garrick Do not alarm yourself, Doctor!

Johnson I am not alarmed. I am mortally terrified!

Garrick (*calling*) Mrs Butler!

Johnson It is the pall of my melancholy, Davy, that has fallen across me.

Mrs Butler hurries in.

Garrick Take the Doctor here on a short walk, Mrs Butler. His nerves are troubling him.

Mrs Butler He's very large, Mr Garrick. What if he tries to escape?

Johnson Madam, there is no escape.

Garrick Perhaps exercise, sir, will refresh your memory. (*Garrick returns to rehearsal with knife.*)

> By the immortal destiny that dooms
> Me to this cursed minute
> I'll not live one longer.

Peg Woffington enters.

Woffington Hold, sir, be patient. Drury Lane just had one manager croak on them, we don't want another.

Garrick It's not for personal use, you understand.

Woffington I'm here because you want to destroy me.

Garrick Don't go all dramatic on me.

Woffington To take away my work.

Garrick That is a typical Woffington overreaction.

Woffington That is a typical Garrick obfuscation.

Garrick It's standard practice for a new manager to create a new repertoire.

Woffington With none of my parts in it.

Garrick We will, of course, be looking at new ways of including you in the season. This isn't personal.

Woffington You still love me and out of sheer bitterness you want to destroy me.

Garrick Peg, I'm about to be a happily married man.

Woffington I've met a lot of those.

Garrick I know. I made a list of all your misdemeanours. I found it the other day and had a good laugh.

Woffington I suppose you were clearing things out.

Garrick My wife and I will be moving into our new home.

Woffington You're not clearing me out of the theatre. Why have you cut *The Constant Couple*? Nobody does Sir Harry like I do. I've got the legs for it. (*She shows her legs.*)

Garrick Put those away.

Woffington They're only legs. Nothing to be scared of. You've seem them before.

Garrick If Sir Harry Wildair gets done again, he won't be played by a woman.

Woffington Why not? I made that part.

Garrick It is now considered vulgar for a woman to play a man.

Woffington Don't be a prick.

Garrick Unfortunately there are a lot of pricks that think the same way and they buy the tickets.

Woffington So what if I show my legs? Theatre isn't church. If it was, people would stop going.

Garrick Your theatre is finished. People are eager for change and I want to give it to them. Emotion, not cynicism. Dignity, not immorality.

Woffington I bet you never fucked her yet, have you?

Garrick No, because she's been well brought up.

Woffington I'd rather come from the gutter than from genteel poverty like you, forever sewing pockets over holes. I'd rather go naked.

Garrick Which you do with great frequency.

Woffington I don't know why God gave you your talent, because it's wasted on you. Always bowing and scraping and scared of what you want.

Garrick I got what I wanted.

Woffington Bastard. (*She picks up a knife.*)

Garrick That's retractable.

Woffington Typical. When I chose you, you ran off. That's what I don't understand – how you started out brave and ended up a coward.

Garrick After two years of putting up with you and your numerous infidelities, are you suggesting I should have stayed?

Woffington My lovers gave you an excuse. You wanted this theatre, not me.

Garrick Yes, I was tired of your world and its casual humiliations. It was cruel.

Mrs Cibber enters.

Mrs Cibber Mr Garrick?

Woffington I'll go to Dublin; the management there has a bit of sense. My life from now on doesn't look so bad: twenty-seven, beautiful, the toast of the Dublin stage. Yours looks a lot worse: married to a virgin and arse-licking your way around London.

Garrick Mrs Woffington is leaving us, Susannah. (*to Peg*) May I offer you the usual sentiments?

Woffington Shove your sentiments.

Mrs Cibber Mr Garrick is careful to preserve the appearance of a dignified exchange. Some of us have a reputation to lose.

Woffington Yes, and some of us have a face like a dog's arse. Goodbye, Mr Garrick, I hope you suffocate. (*She exits.*)

Mrs Cibber I've come to congratulate you, Mr Garrick, on your accession as manager.

Garrick Now Mrs Woffington is leaving us, Susannah, Drury Lane needs you more than ever.

Mrs Cibber I appear to have several new and demanding roles.

Garrick You are our leading actress, Mrs Cibber.

Mrs Cibber That's wonderful, although I may have to spend a few months in the country later in the season.

Garrick That's extremely inconvenient.

Mrs Cibber Yes. I've explained everything in this letter.

She hands him the letter. He takes it impatiently and reads silently. He looks up slowly.

Garrick A woman's condition? Well, I suppose congratulations are in order.

Mrs Cibber Not really. My first husband and I don't live as man and wife and my second husband is seventy-two.

Garrick Good Lord.

Mrs Cibber Yes, you can say that again. It really is the most frightful situation. But you were very distressed that day you left Mrs Woffington. Your acting advice took an unexpected turn.

Garrick Are you sure?

Mrs Cibber I shall spend a month in the country and then we must continue as if nothing ever happened. I know what it's like to live in the wilderness, Mr Garrick, and you would not take to it. And if you were not here, I could not be.

Garrick Yes, yes, I see. I suppose it's the thing to do.

Mrs Cibber Before I go, may I say that I look forward to our playing in *King John* together. I am to be Lady

Constance. I understand you had some concerns about me. I was primarily a musical person.

Garrick I have great hopes of your success. Even though your voice is naturally soft and inaudible.

Mrs Cibber Thank you. I wonder if I might steal a moment of your time. It concerns Lady Constance's screams of maternal agony at the loss of her son. Might I be allowed to ask what you think of the one I've been practising at home?

Garrick Very well.

Mrs Cibber Here goes.

She does a blood-curdlingly impressive scream.

Garrick That will do very well.

Mrs Cibber Mr Garrick.

She exits. Garrick sits silently for a moment. Johnson reappears with Goldsmith and Mrs Butler.

Mrs Butler He is restored, Mr Garrick.

Johnson I have it! The Prologue. And look who I bumped into, a young acquaintance of mine, a Dr Goldsmith. He has literary ambitions, like most Irishmen.

Mrs Butler He is rather foolish and has no money, but he seemed to lift the Doctor's spirits. It must be that to discover a fellow worse off than ourselves is in some way cheering.

Goldsmith I'm delighted that the theatre will b–be undergoing a renaissance in your hands, Mr Garrick. I look forward to the future with great interest.

Johnson
Hard is his lot that here by fortune placed
Must watch the wild vicissitudes of taste,

73

With every meteor of caprice must play
And chase the new-blown bubbles of the day.

Garrick takes over. The rest exit.

Garrick
Ah! Let not censure term our fate, our choice,
The stage but echoes back the public voice.
The drama's laws, the drama's patrons give,
For we that live to please must please to live.

Hannah More enters, carrying a small tray of tea.

Hannah Mrs Garrick has sent me over with some tea.

Garrick Thank you, Hannah.

She sets up tea things. She looks at what he is reading.

Hannah Have you reached a decision yet, Mr Garrick?

Garrick I think Drury Lane may be ready to take its comedy a little raw.

Hannah Oh.

Garrick I sense the town has grown a little disenchanted with weeping comedy. I've determined to give them a laugh. Being one step ahead, Hannah, is the secret of good theatre management.

Hannah But isn't there a danger of a scandal with Dr Goldsmith's play?

Garrick Scandal? No. I think I can risk a little disapproval at my age.

Hannah I hope you don't mind me speaking out. But I find Reverend Cumberland's play to have such elegant sentiments and elevated behaviour.

Garrick They are not much fun to act, Hannah.

Hannah But what is the point of Dr Goldsmith's play?

Why should we want to see such characters on stage? They don't instruct us in decent behaviour. Art must have moral purpose, Mr Garrick. That's how God and art fit together.

Garrick I cannot believe that God has anything to do with some of the horrors that land on my desk.

Hannah When I walked here that morning, Mr Garrick, I once or twice discerned bundles at the roadside. Desiring to rest a little, I found myself beside one. It was a baby. Frozen.

Garrick It's a sad fact, Hannah.

Hannah How did those girls get their babies in the first place?

Garrick Perhaps Mrs Garrick . . .

Hannah Their morals, I meant. Reverend Cumberland's play cultivates a refined sensibility, encourages us to aspire to a life of decency and beauty. What is life without beauty? And would Mr Cautherley be Tony Lumpkin?

Garrick I'd rather he played Marlow, but I want to encourage him.

Hannah But would it be beneficial to him, Mr Garrick? He's a young gentleman with his future before him. I found this. (*She brings out a letter.*)

Garrick What is it?

Hannah A letter. From Mrs Cibber.

Garrick That's ancient history. There's a fire in the green room. That's the place for it.

Hannah Reverend Cumberland's play is so wonderfully fresh and unjaded. So full of hope for a new future.

Garrick Yes, yes, that's true. That's a very thoughtful argument, thank you, Hannah.

Hannah Would you like sugar, Mr Garrick?

Garrick Six, please, Hannah.

Hannah I feel privileged to have had a chance to influence history, Mr Garrick. It brings me a little closer to you. (*She exits.*)

SCENE TWO

Johnson Melancholy. A disease supposed to proceed from an abundance of black bile. A kind of madness in which the mind is always fixed on one object. A gloomy, pensive, disenchanted temper.

The Turk's Head. A late stage in the proceedings.

Goldsmith So, sirs, in conclusion. There has never been an actor that combined such a happy facility to move and excite as Mr Garrick.

Boswell Goldy has had a change of heart.

Goldsmith He is unab–bated excellence!

Boswell He has had a complete change of personality.

Goldsmith And although he is small, he can dwarf the stage at will. That is his genius.

Johnson That is his platform shoes. Acting is nothing but trickery, sir; do not be taken in by it.

Boswell We must allow a great player some merit.

Johnson What, sir, a fellow who claps a hump on his back and cries, 'I am Richard the Third.' Nay, sir, a ballad-singer is a higher man, for he does two things: he repeats and he sings.

Boswell You can turn anything to ridicule, sir.

Burke Mankind has agreed in admiring talents for the stage. A great player does what very few are capable of. His art is a rare faculty.

Reynolds Who can repeat Hamlet's soliloquy, 'To be or not to be,' as Garrick does it?

Johnson Anybody may. The tea boy may do it as well in a week.

Reynolds He will not be paid one thousand pounds a year for it. That is a proof of great acting.

Johnson Is getting a thousand pounds a proof of excellence? That has been got by scoundrels.

Boswell I allow that a player of farce is not entitled to respect, but he who can represent exalted characters has very respectable powers.

Goldsmith But represents only half of human nature. Mr Garrick is more democratic. In my play he will be playing some farce.

Johnson Garrick has lived with more splendour than is suitable to a player and thinks only of fine company, not of his friends.

Repulsive Old Man enters.

Old Man Excuse me, sirs, you expect one Garrick?

Boswell For the last hour, old man.

Old Man Well, he's not coming.

Johnson How are you privy to this confidence, sir?

Old Man I'm his hairdresser.

Reynolds Clearly a walking advertisement.

Old Man Point me in the right direction I can work wonders with a comb and scissors. I have an intelligence from Mr Garrick, if I can lay my hands upon it. (*He searches, finds it.*) 'To the Turk's Head club. A group of learned and ingenious men who meet to further the advancement of culture.' How do I know I have the right group?

Johnson You may take myself sir, Dr Samuel Johnson, as proof. I am only likely to make my companions men of sense.

Old Man You certainly have the Doctor's appearance. A boat of a man with crumpled stockings and a singed wig.

Reynolds It is a litigious old fellow.

Johnson Proceed, sir, what have you for us?

Old Man (*reads*) 'Sirs, forgive me. I have been called from London on unexpected business and must forego the pleasure of your company.' Read, sirs: he's had a better offer.

Burke You have no high opinion of your employer?

Old Man Has anybody?

Goldsmith P–perhaps it is the case that he has been called from London. Garrick is an extremely important man with a great deal of b–business to attend to.

Old Man blows his nose on a rag and wipes in on his sleeve.

Old Man Your name, sir?

Goldsmith Oliver Goldsmith.

Old Man I suppose you've not had the news, sir.

Goldsmith The news?

Old Man That Mr Garrick has passed your play over, sir. I have the playbill here. *The Fashionable Lover* – some veritable twaddle – opens on Tuesday.

Boswell I'll have to get tickets for that.

Reynolds Have a heart, Bozzy.

Goldsmith The b–backsliding b–bastard. Has Mr Garrick made clear his reasons?

Old Man Mr Garrick says your play mocks gentility, sir.

Goldsmith It mocks its affectations.

Old Man I have no time for affectations, sir. For example, you, sir, are ugly.

Goldsmith Very true.

Old Man Your coat is ugly.

Goldsmith I'd b–beg to disagree on that one.

Burke No, it is ugly.

Reynolds We are all profoundly sorry for you, Goldy.

Old Man Your wig is also quite repulsive. Yesterday I saw a dead dog, it is as if you had picked it up and placed it on your head, but only at the back.

Reynolds Hold off, old man.

Old Man Garrick is always huffing and puffing about politeness – he would consider it bad form to comment upon your coiffure in such a manner, but I stand up for the liberty of the Englishman to insult his neighbour.

Burke Without manners, sir, we are little more than beasts!

Old Man I was an actor once. I had a superlative act. I burped the alphabet while juggling five dogs. But Mr Garrick, sir, would have nothing of it. For it was too low.

Burke Indeed, old man, your act sounds quite missable.

Old Man I have heard him call Dr Goldsmith's play low. But what of that! What is so very wrong with the low?

(*He farts.*) Pardon. Just because his play has a man fondling a woman at every opportunity! If a man's parts cannot rise in the theatre at the sight of an actress having her bubbies squeezed, it is a sad day.

Goldsmith I was making a political point.

The Old Man scratches his balls.

Old Man Make as many of them as you like.

Goldsmith (*to Old Man*) I wish you would not argue for me, sir, you are not scoring me any points.

Burke The master of the theatre, as Garrick is, is a kind of general trustee for the nation. He holds in ward the morals of a rising race of people. Their manners, prejudices, gallantries and deportment must take deep impression from his conduct. Take this man, gentlemen. (*He indicates Old Man.*) What an execrable creature.

Old Man I'll do a bit of my act, if you like. (*burping*) A . . . B . . . C . . .

Burke Imagine him as a road. A road leading backwards to decline and chaos. Imagine him as a play! Garrick chose not to take that path and must be commended.

Goldsmith Look at him again, gentlemen. Is there not something human in him? That invites us to look at ourselves? Ridiculous pride in his burps and his dogs. He doesn't see that he damages the very cause he wishes to promote. We laugh at the faults in him and so correct them in ourselves.

Johnson After all, it is the end of comedy to make us merry.

Reynolds The danger is, to show such vulgarity is to encourage its emulation.

Goldsmith There is no danger in him!

Old Man Thank you, sir. I shall offer you a haircut on the house. (*The Old Man advances towards Goldsmith.*)

Goldsmith No, thank you.

Old Man grabs him.

Goldsmith Unhand me, sir. He has a grip of iron!

Reynolds Shake him off, Goldy.

Goldsmith I cannot. That is my eyebrow.

Old Man It will grow back.

Goldsmith Help!

Johnson Sir, it should be clear to any sensible member of your profession that your services are no longer required.

Boswell It appears there is great danger in a fool!

Garrick You make excellent sense, sir, as always.

Boswell It is Mr Garrick, how marvellous!

Reynolds Good Lord!

Goldsmith Garrick!

Garrick I had no hope of a hearing, sirs, I live in fear of the retribution of writers and so came in disguise.

Boswell A most amazing demonstration of your powers. Are you not amazed, Dr Johnson?

Johnson Nothing Davy does amazes me.

Goldsmith My hair does not resemble a dead dog.

Boswell It does now.

Goldsmith Your intention was to make a fool of me.

Garrick My intention, sir, was to show that there is some merit in aspiring to gentility and refinement. I wished to demonstrate that there is an argument to be had against vulgarity.

Goldsmith It was not kind.

Burke But comedy is not kind, sir. That is Mr Garrick's contention, which he has proved admirably.

Goldsmith Very good, sir, I am a figure of fun.

Johnson Which is why we tolerate your company. May we say at last the topic of your play is dead? I have done my best for you, Goldy, and now you must be stoic. When life is not getting worse, it is generally unhappy.

Boswell Let us toast Mr Garrick.

Johnson I shall toast Goldy.

Reynolds That is not consistent, sir.

Johnson There is no great value in consistency. One may be consistently wrong. I desire to toast the loser for a change. That is the Englishman in me.

Goldsmith B–b–but I am not necessarily the loser, Doctor. I have a letter here from Mr Colman at Covent Garden. Hearing that Mr Garrick was to do my p–play he b–begs that I return it to him on promise of a production. I shall do so immediately. I second the toast to myself.

All Dr Goldsmith!

Reynolds Why, it will be something of a competition, Mr Garrick. The two plays simultaneously.

All drink except Garrick.

SCENE THREE: IN-YER-FACE THEATRE

Garrick's office. Cautherley is waiting. Hannah comes in.

Hannah Mr Garrick has decided to do *The Fashionable Lover.*

Cautherley Yes.

Hannah You could seem a little more cheerful, Mr Cautherley. Perhaps I could help you with your lines.

Cautherley No, thank you.

Hannah Mrs Garrick thinks you'll do very well. She's very fond of you. She's always talking about you. Your eyes, your hair, the way it flops down onto your forehead. You've got strong legs. Your hands. You're very sensitive, she says. She likes you. She wouldn't be surprised if the whole audience fell in love with you.

Cautherley Hmmm.

Hannah Charles Millward is a wonderful part.

Cautherley Is it?

Hannah He's tortured by his feelings and he struggles to find a way to express them. He longs to marry Augusta but he can't because she's too poor and so he struggles with duty and longing and he struggles all the time – he's always struggling but he can never put it into words. She's struggling too. She's in love with him but she mustn't say it or it would compromise his struggle so she struggles not to make his struggle more of a struggle. It's a struggle.

Cautherley He's a cunt.

Hannah I don't know what that is, Mr Cautherley, but I don't like the sound of it.

Cautherley Kiss me again.

Hannah I don't know what you're talking about. There won't be any more of that. That's why I begged Mr Garrick not to do *She Stoops to Conquer*.

Cautherley You did!

Hannah I know you won't like me now I've told you that, but I don't care what you think of me. That play is ugly. It insists on mocking refinement. You have no idea, Mr Cautherley, of the joys of sensibility. I feel sorry for you. Do you see this flower?

Cautherley Yes.

Hannah I feel with this flower the heat of sun on its petals. The delicate roundness of a drop of dew, the bright garden throbbing with intensity around it.

Cautherley takes the flower and eats it.

Hannah Why did you do that?

Cautherley Just a joke.

Hannah Lumpkin!

Garrick enters.

Hannah Mr Garrick. (*She exits.*)

Garrick So, Mr Cautherley, how are you finding theatrical life?

Cautherley All right, thank you, Mr Garrick.

Garrick Drury Lane has to be good tonight, Mr Cautherley. *She Stoops to Conquer* opens at Covent Garden. We want to take the laurels.

Cautherley I don't see how we can, Mr Garrick.

Garrick Now don't take that attitude. We've no choice in the matter. We must sell the play to the audience. It must appear as if we relish every word. That way we convince them it's a masterpiece.

Cautherley But I know you to be a good judge of plays, sir. I don't understand.

Garrick Let me worry about my judgement. Now, let's see what Mrs Butler has to say about how you've been doing. (*He opens ledger.*) Tuesday 8th September. *Macbeth.* Mr Cautherley fit of giggles on seeing beards of witches. Failure to exit. Friday 11th. *Antony and Cleopatra.* Mr Cautherley forgets to bring on asp. Cleopatra suffocates herself with pillow.

Cautherley I don't think anybody noticed.

Garrick Saturday 12th. Lines lost. Cautherley makes up bollocks. And so on. Ah, Wednesday 9th. Mr Cautherley rendered inaudible by squeaking. Can you explain that to me?

Cautherley That wasn't my fault. Macklin let rip the most enormous fart.

Garrick If it's not in the play, it hasn't happened.

Cautherley But it did happen and the first ten rows can stand me witness.

Garrick When I was your age, I walked to London with sixpence in my pocket. I hung around the theatre till they thought I was part of the furniture. I would have died and gone to heaven if I'd had half the opportunities you've had. Now I know you have promise, sir, and I don't like to be proved wrong. So what is it that makes you fail so miserably? Let's start with Charles Millward.

Cautherley I don't like him, Mr Garrick.

Garrick What's wrong with him?

Cautherley He's in love all the time.

Garrick He's the romantic lead, Mr Cautherley. People want to feel for somebody when they come to the theatre.

Cautherley Lumpkin. I could have played that part, Mr Garrick. I had a feeling for it.

Garrick I have made my decision. Trust me. You are better appearing as a young gentleman.

Cautherley You mean because I do not know my parents.

Garrick You have become a gentleman, sir, through your character, as I have. That is why I recommend you leave the Lumpkins of this world well alone.

Cautherley At school, sir, because I was no one they treated me accordingly.

Garrick Well, that was very bad, sir.

Cautherley I used to dream of some way to get back at them. Lumpkin does that.

Garrick I am sorry you were not happy at school, Sam, but I cannot programme my theatre to satisfy a boyhood grudge. You do see that?

Cautherley I know I am indebted to you.

Garrick Yes.

Cautherley I was very grateful to come to you in the holidays, sir. I remember you impersonated a turkey.

Garrick Did I?

Cautherley And a drunk, and Mrs Garrick.

Garrick I still do a very good Mrs Garrick.

Cautherley I only ever laughed when I was at your house. I remembered what you did and then I did it for the boys at school. I used to pretend I was your son, sir. Perhaps if I was I would not exercise you as I do.

Garrick We live in a world where we cannot always do as we wish. People think I'll be selling the patent, but I'd like to pass this place on to a friend. I'm looking for that friend all the time, eh, Sam? Charles Millward is just one part. There'll be others you like better. Study hard, my boy, for seven years, and you may play the rest of your life.

Cautherley Yes, Mr Garrick.

Garrick So, tonight?

Cautherley I won't let you down, sir.

Garrick Good lad.

Cautherley exits.

Johnson Patron. One who countenances, supports or protects. Commonly a wretch who supports with insolence and is paid with flattery.

SCENE FOUR

Backstage, Drury Lane.

Macklin These costumes, Mrs Butler.

Mrs Butler Yes, Mr Macklin?

Macklin They're a little overdone.

Mrs Butler It says 'fashionable' in the title, Mr Macklin.

Mrs Cibber It's too late to do anything about it now.

Mrs Butler The greater emphasis on design in contemporary theatre is due to paucity of content and you can't blame me for that. I only do the sewing.

Macklin Why am I covered in fur?

Mrs Butler You were abroad for many years. Five minutes, please. (*She exits.*)

Mrs Cibber Have you seen Mr Cautherley? Ah, here he is.

    Cautherley enters.

We're on in ten minutes.

Cautherley Yes. There are a great many lines to remember.

Mrs Barry One opens one's mouth and they come out.

Barry They didn't come out in rehearsal.

Cautherley It's the last scene I'm shaky on.

Barry You're home and dry by the last scene, love. I'd worry about getting there.

Macklin I share your concerns, sir, I'm expiring under the weight of dead animal.

Mrs Cibber Set his mind at rest, Mr Macklin. Go through his last scene with him.

Cautherley I'd be grateful, sir.

Mrs Barry I'm in your arms, I think.

Barry He said the lines, Lavinia.

Mrs Cibber Let us be quick about it.

Macklin Very well, we enter. (*He says the lines – a speed version.*) Give me thy hand Augusta. I was labouring for thy sake that I should restore the prostrate fortunes of an ancient house. I have toiled through eighteen years of wearisome adventure, crowned with success. I now return and find my daughter all my fondest hope could represent. I now bestow my treasure in faithful hands. What say you sir? Will you accept the charge?

They all look at Cautherley. A pause.

Mrs Barry That's your line, Mr Cautherley.

Barry There's a clue when he says, 'What say you, sir?'

Cautherley What do I say?

All You say, 'Yes.'

Cautherley Yes.

Garrick enters with Lady Kingston.

Garrick Company, let me call you together for a moment. Our patron would like to address us.

Lady Kingston So these are the actors. How fascinating.

They bow/curtsey.

Lady Kingston I would love to know something of the authentic behind-the-scenes life.

Garrick I'm sure we would be happy to oblige you.

Lady Kingston How splendid. And you all regard one another as family, I expect.

All Yes.

Lady Kingston I suppose because you work as an ensemble it is the greater good that motivates you.

All Yes.

Macklin When you get to my age, Your Grace, you realise that work is the only thing and you regret all the hours you have wasted in taverns.

Mrs Cibber When did you realise that, Mr Macklin?

Garrick Ha ha ha . . .

Lady Kingston Mr Garrick, you must be congratulated upon your excellent company.

Garrick Your Grace.

Lady Kingston I know I shall have good reason to be proud of you all and my association with Drury Lane.

Garrick We are deeply grateful for your interest, madam.

Cumberland As the author, I have prepared a short speech, which I propose . . .

Lady Kingston Nobody cares about that, Cumberland. Come on.

They exit.

Garrick Break a leg, everybody.

All Break a leg, Mr Garrick.

Mrs Butler (*off*) Scene One – beginners, Mr Macklin, Mr Garrick, Mr Barry.

They exit.

Mrs Cibber I'm not on for twenty-seven minutes.

Mrs Barry What's the house like, Mrs Butler?

Mrs Butler There's a good crowd in. Quite a few vicars.

Mrs Cibber That's always a comforting thought.

Mrs Butler And a smattering of minor Royals.

Mrs Barry I shall play to them.

Mrs Butler Don't let Mr Garrick catch you.

Mrs Barry I won't do it when he's on.

Mrs Cibber approaches Mr Cautherley.

Mrs Cibber Mr Cautherley. If there's any advice I can give you in a professional capacity, please don't hesitate to ask.

Cautherley That's very kind, Mrs Cibber.

Mrs Cibber I'm an old hand.

Cautherley You're a very fine actress. I can only apologise for what happened with your Cleopatra. I keep wanting to laugh in the love bits.

Mrs Cibber My advice is to remember a time you were in love. Bring those feelings to mind and that will assist you in playing the part.

Cautherley I'm not sure I've ever been in love.

Mrs Cibber You surprise me, Mr Cautherley.

Cautherley Once I found a bird.

Mrs Cibber A bird?

Cautherley In the school grounds. I took it back to my room, but the next morning it was quite stiff.

Mrs Cibber And this is what you bring to mind when you are making passionate love to Miss Aubrey?

Cautherley Yes.

Mrs Cibber You must stop it at once. You must think of a person.

Cautherley grabs Mrs Cibber and kisses her passionately.

Mrs Cibber Mr Cautherley, I am out of the question.

Cautherley Why? I'll never be able to think of anyone else in time.

Mrs Butler Mr Cautherley, Mrs Barry.

They exit. A shout heard off. They listen. Re-enter Macklin.

Mrs Butler How is it, Mr Macklin?

Macklin A faction in the gallery doesn't appreciate characters of Scottish descent.

Mrs Butler Only the gallery. That's not bad.

Enter Reverend Cumberland.

Cumberland Perhaps you could tone down the accent, Mr Macklin.

Macklin With a name like Hamish Macleod?

A louder jeer: 'No Scots! No foreigners!'

Mrs Butler You've a fair number of foreigners in your play, Reverend Cumberland.

Cumberland That is intentional, ma'am.

Mrs Butler It is trouble, sir.

Mrs Cibber The boxes support the French.

Macklin The gallery loathes them.

Mrs Butler The middle are caught in the middle.

Macklin No one supports the Scottish. It's a daft idea to have them in a play in the first place.

Mrs Butler Mr Macklin!

He begins to exit.

Cumberland Try smiling more, Mr Macklin!

Mrs Butler It is all an excuse for them to hate each other.

Mrs Cibber The pit hate the gallery.

Mrs Butler The boxes hate the pit.

Mrs Cibber The gallery hates everybody.

Mrs Butler And everybody hates the Scots.

Cumberland This is the very point my play addresses. Feeling with a person encourages us to transcend superficial differences.

Cautherley re-enters with Garrick.

Garrick How was that, Mr Cautherley?

Cautherley Someone called me a French arse. It was when I said I'd engaged in a contretemps.

Garrick You're doing extremely well, Mr Cautherley. And all of you.

Barry They said I was French, too, Mr Garrick, but I'm not, am I?

Garrick You should know, Mr Barry.

Barry You've got to tell them I've never been further than Barnstaple.

Mrs Cibber Du Barry is a French name. Perhaps they're a little confused?

Barry I'm scared, Mr Garrick.

Garrick Calm down, Mr Barry. There'll be a few cuts tomorrow.

Cumberland Ahh . . . cuts . . .

Mrs Butler Mr Garrick!

Cumberland follows Garrick off.

Cumberland I don't quite see the necessity. We mustn't give up on it too early . . .

He exits. Mrs Barry enters.

Mrs Barry I've handled them!

Barry Yes, Lavinia, and so have half the audience.

Mrs Butler Mr Barry. Stage right.

He exits.

Mr Cautherley, Mrs Barry. Stage left.

They exit.

Hopefully we can now have a nice quiet night of it.

Sounds of jeering increase to a roar. A loud crash. Mrs Butler and Mrs Cibber react. Cautherley is brought on unconscious, carried by Garrick and Barry. Mr Barry is carrying a potato. Mrs Cibber gasps.

Mrs Cibber Will he be all right?

Garrick Put him here.

Mrs Barry He's out cold.

Mrs Barry It was a potato that struck him on the head, Mr Garrick.

Barry It was this potato here. They threw one at me too, Lavinia.

Mrs Barry I'll loosen his clothing.

Barry Lavinia!

Cautherley mumbles.

Garrick Do you know who I am, son?

Cautherley Mr Garrick.

Garrick Thank God.

Mrs Cibber Thank goodness.

Barry Yes, they threw one at me, too, Mr Garrick, but I ducked.

Garrick Good for you, Mr Barry. Your reflexes were working for once. The audience is a little restive tonight. They will subside shortly and we will continue with our performance.

94

A roar.

Cautherley Is it my line?

Mrs Cibber Poor Mr Cautherley. He can't go on. Mrs Butler must do it with the book.

Cautherley (*to Mrs Cibber*) Who are you?

Mrs Cibber Mrs Cibber, a fellow actor.

Cautherley You seem familiar. As if I knew you.

Mrs Cibber Mr Garrick, he has such a strange look in his eyes.

Garrick Not now, Susannah.

Macklin enters with a cauliflower.

Have you anything fresh to report, Mr Macklin?

Macklin Yes. A man has manoeuvred himself onto the chandelier and has commandeered vegetable projectiles.

Garrick What else did you ascertain?

Macklin I ascertained that a discerning minority of the audience are fed up with *The Fashionable Lover* and are creating their own entertainment diverting themselves with anti-French feeling and nationalistic fervour.

Mrs Cibber I'm sure the religious gentlemen are getting a great deal from the performance.

Macklin Last thing was they have set about the anti-French faction with cushions.

Garrick Cushions?

Macklin Untimely ripped from the new seating arrangements.

Garrick Good God.

Macklin Yes, Mr Garrick, you have a riot on your hands.

Mrs Butler A lot of what people enjoy about the theatre is riots.

A loud crash.

That'll be the chandelier.

Garrick Six hundred pounds. I'll have to go and speak to them.

Mrs Cibber It might not be safe.

Garrick I cannot let them tear the theatre apart, Mrs Cibber.

Garrick exits. Cumberland re-enters.

Cumberland What is it that offends them?

All The French.

Macklin The play is unrelieved by laughter. They have no outlet for hatred and have turned on each other.

Mrs Cibber You wouldn't think religious gentlemen could make such a mess of a cushion.

Loud jeers and chanting from audience: 'Monsieur! Monsieur! On your knees, Garrick! Apologise! Pardon, pardon!'

Cumberland He doesn't appear to be winning them over.

Macklin There is nothing for it but to call a meeting.

Mrs Butler We haven't done that in years, Mr Macklin.

Macklin The times call for it, Mrs Butler. I declare this meeting of the Drury Lane acting company open. I propose immediate cancellation of this bourgeois frippery.

Mrs Cibber Do we have to bother with all the paraphernalia, Mr Macklin?

Macklin Point of information. Yes.

Mrs Butler Since my promotion I disagree with meetings in principal. I answer only to Mr Garrick.

Macklin Charles Macklin, actor. Presently playing Hamish McLeod. We are in a right turkey.

Mrs Cibber Susannah Cibber, actress. Presently playing bitter spinster of thirty-five. Mr Garrick has just popped out. Can't we wait until he pops back?

Macklin A turkey is a turkey is a turkey.

Cumberland enters chased by two butchers.

Butcher 1 Monsieur, there is no escape!

Cumberland I am beset by butchers. Countrymen, come to my aid.

Butcher 1 We don't want no French fluters!

Butcher 2 We will not suffer these foreign dogs to amuse us!

Cumberland O Britons!

He exits pursued by the butchers.

Barry Mr Barry, actor. Has anyone got the key to the back door?

All No.

Barry I thought it was going to be all right at first. I got a laugh when I came on.

Mrs Butler Point of information. It was the costume that got a laugh, Mr Barry.

Mrs Barry Anyway, now they want to kill you.

Barry I'm not voting against the management, it's old-fashioned.

Macklin You'd do it quick enough if you had to go out there and apologise.

Barry Mr Garrick wouldn't do that. This is the eighteenth century.

Garrick re-enters. Cries of 'No French, no Scottish! No foreigners! Pardon! Pardon!'

Mrs Cibber Here is Mr Garrick.

Garrick Mr Barry. It might help if you declare yourself an Englishman.

Barry I vote with you, Mr Macklin.

Garrick There's nothing to be afraid of, Spranger. If you apologise for sounding French, the show can continue.

Barry I have withdrawn my labour, Mr Garrick, and so has Lavinia.

Macklin And so have we all, pending the cancellation of *The Fashionable Lover.*

Mrs Butler It is mutiny, Mr Garrick.

Garrick Lady Kingston has been signalling me from the royal box. She is greatly anxious for the show to continue.

Barry (*pointing to Cautherley*) It's him they want. Charles Millwood. It's because he does French things with his glove.

Mrs Butler That's right, Mr Garrick.

Cautherley I'm happy to face them, sir.

Mrs Cibber The poor boy is not himself . . .

Macklin He has been struck by a vegetable, which I cite as evidence supporting my proposal.

Garrick Mr Cautherley has graciously agreed to apologise to the audience for their misapprehension. I'll be there with you, Mr Cautherley.

Cautherley Thank you, Mr Garrick.

Butchers re-enter chased by Cumberland and three vicars.

Cumberland This butcher is a bastard!

Butcher 1 You, sir, are a Parisian eunuch!

Vicar Damn you, butchers, your destruction is at hand!

Garrick Gentlemen, settle your differences. Your disturbances are preventing us playing for you.

Cumberland tries to stuff a cushion into the mouth of a butcher.

Cumberland Eat this.

Cumberland exits chased by butcher who is pursued by vicar.

Mrs Cibber There is an untamed mob out there who have failed to be persuaded to good manners. We cannot risk sending Mr Cautherley before them.

Mrs Butler You saw what they did to that cushion.

Garrick Leave this to me, Mrs Butler!

Mrs Cibber My conscience is weighing very heavily on me, Mr Garrick.

Garrick Does it have to be today, Susannah?

Mrs Cibber To let a new company member face the crowd. I would prefer to do it myself.

Barry But you're not French.

Mrs Barry No one is, Mr Barry, or we would send them out there.

Garrick Ready, Mr Cautherley.

Cautherley Yes, Mr Garrick. (*He begins to exit in the wrong direction.*)

Garrick Other way, Mr Cautherley.

Mrs Cibber I won't let you go.

Cautherley But I must, Mrs Cibber.

Mrs Cibber holds on to him, as he begins to exit. A tussle.

Garrick Let him go, Susannah. He's not a child.

She releases him. Cautherley stares at them both.

Macklin I have a suggestion. I have some sketches and impersonations in my repertoire. The material comprises a twenty-minute comic entertainment which would compensate the audience for a dreadful evening in the theatre.

A huge roar.

Mrs Cibber Let them have comedy, Mr Garrick. That is what they deserve.

Banging on door.

Mrs Butler They're at the gates, Mr Garrick!

Macklin Let me go on and entertain them, Mr Garrick.

Garrick Do you do me?

Macklin Not if you say yes.

Garrick Well we have nothing to lose. I'll make the announcement.

Barry What if they still want my blood, Mr Garrick?

Garrick I shall try to resist my impulse to give it to them. If they've objected to Cumberland's play, Covent Garden will be ashes by now. (*Starts to exit.*) Oh and Macklin, make it funny.

Hannah attends to Cautherley's wounds.

Hannah Mr Cautherley, let me see to your head. I've improvised some bandages. My petticoat. You should now spend three days in a darkened room.

SCENE FIVE

Mrs Butler Here's all the Lears we've got.

Garrick Thank you, Mrs Butler. I'm sorry it's such short notice.

Mrs Butler Do you want me to put *The Fashionable Lover* costumes in storage, Mr Garrick?

Garrick Put them where you like, Mrs Butler. (*He goes behind screen and tries on costume.*)

Mrs Butler I expect you're glad to get back to the classics, Mr Garrick? They tend to be less trouble than new plays.

Garrick Yes, and you can trust that the theatre will still be standing at the end of the evening. That's one show report I could do without.

Mrs Butler You'll have to, Mr Garrick. Somebody shat in the prompt book.

He emerges as Lear, with beard, staff and robe.

Mrs Butler Very nice, Mr Garrick. Shall we see how it looks on stage?

Cautherley enters with bandaged head.

Garrick I'll be with you shortly, Mrs Butler.

She exits.

Mr Cautherley?

Cautherley I thought you said people wanted to see characters like Mr Millward, sir.

Garrick Last night was one incident, it doesn't prove me wrong.

Cautherley But Dr Goldsmith's play is a great success.

Enter Goldsmith and Johnson. They sing:

Goldsmith/Johnson
Let schoolmasters puzzle their brain
With grammar and nonsense and learning,
Good liquor I stoutly maintain
Gives reason a better discerning.

Goldsmith We haven't been to bed.

Johnson We have seen the sun, like a great eye, open.

Goldsmith B–but we haven't come to gloat.

Johnson Small men gloat.

Goldsmith Large men like ourselves, what do we do?

Johnson Wayzgoose.

Goldsmith Exactly.

Johnson We witnessed a death, Davy. Sentimental drama was mortally wounded.

Goldsmith They laughed!

Johnson I had to give them a bit of help at first.

Goldsmith He roared like a rhino. It is very b–bad manners to celebrate in so public a fashion, b–but I can't help it.

Johnson How was your night, Davy?

Garrick I've had better.

Cautherley May I congratulate you on the success of your play, Dr Goldsmith?

Goldsmith You may, sir, as much as you like.

Garrick You may have my congratulations too, Doctor. Weeping comedy was never to my personal taste.

Cautherley Does this mean, sir, that low comedy is now in fashion?

Garrick I will never touch comedy again. My final weeks will be for the great tragic roles. They end in death. People are humbled and don't go tearing up the seating arrangements.

Johnson There was an excellent moment, Davy, in Goldy's play, where Hardcastle tells of a battle and no one will listen to him for they think he is a servant . . . ha . . . ha . . . ha . . .

Goldsmith That's a great moment.

Garrick Perhaps you will excuse me, gentlemen. We have a very busy morning.

Goldsmith Let us spread the good news, Doctor.

They exit singing:

Let schoolmasters puzzle their brain
With grammar and nonsense and learning . . .

Garrick Mr Cautherley?

Cautherley Yes, Mr Garrick?

Garrick Are you fit for tonight's performance?

Cautherley Yes, sir.

Garrick Good lad.

Cautherley I'm playing Edmund, sir, the bastard.

Garrick I know that, sir.

Cautherley Although he does know who his father is.

Garrick Yes.

Cautherley He seems to live with his father, sir, in the same house.

Garrick Yes.

Cautherley His father even seems to make a joke of it. 'His breeding sir, hath been at my charge. I have so often blushed to acknowledge him that I am now brazed to it.' It's very different, sir, from today.

Garrick We've moved on a little.

Cautherley 'I grow, I prosper, now gods stand up for bastards!'

Garrick Yes, not so loud, Mr Cautherley.

Cautherley At least he knew who his father was, sir. An earl. I shouldn't mind an earl in the least. Mrs Butler says it was actors.

Garrick Have you your costume for this evening, sir? Mrs Butler's very exercised today.

Cautherley Yes, Mr Garrick.

Cautherley exits. Garrick swigs some of his medicine. Macklin climbs out of the skip, dressed as a woman.

Macklin Mr Garrick, have you got a moment?

Garrick Good God, Mr Macklin!

Macklin A small difficulty has arisen. I have to flee the country. And so I'd be grateful for a little advance.

Garrick Explain yourself.

Macklin Last night my sketches were of a satiric nature. Being starved of such fare in the normal run of things, the audience went mad for it and there was a good deal of laughter. Spurred on to boldness by success and your departure from the building, I threw in one final impersonation: Lady Kingston.

Garrick And?

Macklin She's going to kill me. I need money, I need clothes, I need to escape.

Garrick You must stay here until this matter is satisfactorily sorted out. You're playing Gloucester tonight. I'll write a letter of apology to Lady Kingston immediately. Take off those clothes, man.

Macklin (*imitates Lady Kingston*) Thank you kindly, sir. I love nothing more than a forceful rider.

Garrick Enough of that, Mr Macklin.

Garrick exits. Macklin takes off the dress. He hears voice off.

Lady Kingston (*offstage*) Mr Garrick!

Macklin grabs a Lear costume from the bag and dashes behind the screen.

I know you're there, Mr Garrick. Don't think you can hide from me. My tentacles reach to the ends of the earth. I'll have you closed down. Last night Drury Lane hosted a short satiric show by one Charles Macklin.

Macklin (*from behind the screen*) It was quite good, apparently.

Lady Kingston It was poisonous. My person was ridiculed with the aid of a horsewhip. It was slanderously insinuated that I starve my servants and I drink. (*She drinks.*) That I wish my husband dead and have taken a young lover. I demand a public apology. I cannot talk to you behind a screen, Mr Garrick.

A pause. Macklin appears, also dressed as King Lear.

I know you have sympathy with my predicament. You are a respectable man as well as a great actor.

Macklin I'm not that good.

Lady Kingston Nonsense.

Macklin I've just taken all the great parts for myself and not given anyone else a look in.

Lady Kingston Mr Garrick! I demand satisfaction!

Macklin But I'm an old man!

Lady Kingston I need to feel you are behind me in this matter.

Macklin Very well. We'll do it behind the screen.

Lady Kingston The screen?

Macklin Someone might walk in.

Lady Kingston So, that's your price, is it? You loathsome toad! You were with Macklin all the way.

Macklin I've been an admirer ever since his revolutionary Shylock.

Lady Kingston You've never said so before, Mr Garrick. Let's get this over with, shall we?

She goes behind the screen. Macklin hesitates. Hears approach of Garrick and hides back in skip.

Garrick Have you taken the dress off?

Lady Kingston I've barely had a moment, Mr Garrick.

Garrick I find your persistent female impersonation in the worst of taste. Put these on. They'll do for now. (*He thows Lear costume over screen.*)

Lady Kingston Male apparel. Your taste sinks very low.

Garrick It was all I could find. Hurry up. And talk like a man.

Lady Kingston As you wish.

Garrick This whole episode is extremely embarrassing.

Lady Kingston One wonders why you feel impelled to go through with it.

Garrick There are some duties one must perform even though they are abhorrent. I have business with Mrs Butler.

Lady Kingston Her too!

Garrick exits. Macklin climbs out of skip and makes to escape, but Lady Kingston comes out from behind the screen, also dressed as Lear.

You are dragging this out most unpleasantly. We could have had this over and done with in five minutes if Lord Kingston is anything to go by.

Macklin If 'twere done when 'tis done, then it were well 'twere done quickly.

Lady Kingston Shakespeare too, Mr Garrick. Well, that's a first.

They both go behind screen. Cautherley enters followed by Hannah More. He searches for his costume in the skip.

Cautherley You appear to be following me about.

Hannah I'm concerned for you, Mr Cautherley.

Cautherley It's only a small bump, Miss More.

Hannah I've changed my mind about the theatre, sir. I'd been entertaining a groundless hope that the stage under certain regulations might be converted into a school of virtue. But last night proved me wrong.

Cautherley Mr Garrick says disturbances of that nature are highly unusual.

Hannah Your life was put in danger. The theatre is not the place to reach people. Allow me to convince you, sir, of the waste of life it would be to continue here.

Cautherley Have you seen my costume lying about?

Hannah There's a post advertised in the *Hertfordshire Gazette*, teaching young foundlings. You could come with me, Mr Cautherley.

Cautherley It'll be black. I'm playing Edmund, the bastard.

Hannah Mr Cautherley. I'm trying to save you.

Cautherley I wish you wouldn't bother.

A grunt from behind the screen.

Wait there, Miss More, somebody may be hurt. (*He goes to look behind the screen. He starts visibly.*)

Hannah What is it, Mr Cautherley?

Cautherley Nothing. I think perhaps my head. I need a little air.

He exits. She follows him. A crescendo of grunting behind the screen. Macklin emerges.

Lady Kingston (*from behind screen*) Well, Mr Garrick. Shakespeare is certainly our greatest poet. I now understand your great admiration for him.

Garrick enters. Macklin dives into skip.

Garrick Are you coming yet? You have caused me a good deal of bother.

Lady Kingston I have?

Garrick Indeed. I'm out of breath on your account. I have a very taxing performance ahead of me and I've had to sort you out on top of it.

Lady Kingston It wasn't that bad, was it?

Garrick It was a waste of my time.

Lady Kingston Oh . . .

Garrick I'm sorry for this predicament. I do have a good deal of respect for you. I have indeed admired you for many years.

Lady Kingston Ah . . .

Garrick You have often moved me to tears. *The Provoked Wife, The Careless Husband, The Innocent Mistress*. I am truly sorry to see you brought to this point. I'll compose an apology for you.

Garrick exits. Macklin peeks from skip and, seeing exit clear, tries to escape, but Lady Kingston emerges.

Lady Kingston I am touched, sir. I had not thought there was one who understood my predicament with such sensitivity. I live in a society that punishes a woman's indiscretions mercilessly. Perhaps I have taken a young lover, but so would you if you'd seen my husband. One has to keep one's spirits up somehow.

Macklin I'm not the performer I once was, Lady Kingston.

Lady Kingston You are too modest, Mr Garrick. Let's try the afterpiece in here.

Lady Kingston opens the skip and they both get in, closing the lid on top of them. Enter Hannah and Cautherley. Cautherley shakes his head.

Hannah Does your head feel a little clearer, Mr Cautherley?

Cautherley Yes. Thank you. (*He resumes his search for costume.*)

Hannah Allow me to convince you, sir, of the profound satisfaction to be had in bringing hope to abandoned young children.

Cautherley It's here somewhere.

Hannah Their lives would otherwise be exposed to the brutalities of destitution and misery. Their little faces, Mr Cautherley.

Cautherley I feel very sorry for them, Miss More. But I'm an actor.

Hannah The theatre has not been as kind to you as you think, Mr Cautherley.

Cautherley Miss More, you have been exaggerating profoundly. The theatre is no longer a hotbed of immorality. (*Cautherley opens the skip. He closes it immediately.*)

Hannah What is it?

Cautherley Probably nothing.

Hannah I insist you take another look, Mr Cautherley.

He does so. He starts visibily. Shakes his head.

Hannah Well?

Cautherley I need a little more air, Miss More. I think that potato inflicted more damage than I at first imagined.

He hurries out. She follows him. Garrick enters with letter. He peers behind the screen. He approaches the skip and opens it.

Garrick Good Lord!

Macklin/Lady Kingston Good Lord!

Lady Kingston There are two. Which one is the real Garrick?

Macklin/Garrick I am!

Macklin Lady Kingston, I assure you I am authentic.

Garrick Lady Kingston! Why are you dressed in that fashion?

Lady Kingston I could ask you the same question.

Macklin He is my understudy.

Lady Kingston This is highly misleading. I could have been having the wrong man.

Macklin I assure you, ma'am, I am Garrick.

Lady Kingston Very well. Let us continue.

Enter Johnson, Goldsmith and Mr Larpent. Garrick slams down skip lid.

Johnson Davy, you have an important visitor.

Larpent Where is Garrick?

Garrick I am Garrick.

Larpent I am Mr Larpent, from the Lord Chamberlain's office.

Garrick How do you do, sir.

Larpent Last night Drury Lane staged an impromptu performance lasting twenty minutes which was not submitted for prior inspection to the Lord Chamberlain's office.

Garrick It was a one-off and it won't happen again.

Larpent You broke the law, sir. By rights we could revoke your licence and throw you in gaol.

Garrick I had to calm the audience somehow. Entertaining them seemed the only option.

Larpent That was extremely irresponsible of you, sir.

Garrick I apologise. It won't happen again.

Larpent How is the rest of your programme panning out?

Garrick With tried and tested favourites. *King Lear*, for example.

Larpent You've improved the original, I take it?

Garrick Just a little. It still ends happily.

Larpent Perhaps you'd like to run me through your version.

Garrick It's about a king sir, a venerable old gentleman who made the mistake of having some very bad daughters.

Larpent That sounds inoffensive so far.

Johnson The tragedy of Lear is deservedly celebrated among the dramas of Shakespeare. There is perhaps no play which so much agitates our passions and interests our curiosity.

Goldsmith My play does that too.

Johnson Not now, Goldy.

Cautherley and Hannah More enter.

Hannah Mr Garrick, Mr Cautherley has been seeing things in that basket.

Garrick Perhaps a result of your condition, Mr Cautherley.

Cautherley Two old gentlemen doing things.

Garrick In my theatre I assure you that is not possible.

A noise from the skip.

Larpent There does appear to be something moving in that basket.

Garrick Come out, Mr Macklin. He's a diligent rehearser.

Macklin emerges, still in his Lear costume.

Macklin I'm all rehearsed out, Mr Garrick.

Cautherley There were two, sir!

Garrick Now, Mr Cautherley, remember you are unwell.

Larpent You said there was only one, Mr Garrick!

Macklin I am the old king's identical twin brother.

Larpent Did he have daughters too?

Macklin That's right. They all lived together in a big castle.

Larpent That doesn't necessarily preclude it from performance.

Cautherley Two old fellows going at it like the clappers, Mr Garrick!

Garrick (*to Larpent*) He's been hit on the head by a vegetable.

Larpent We'd all like that excuse. I am trying to establish the suitability of *Lear* for performance. What assurances can you give me?

Lady Kingston emerges. Also as Lear.

Lady Kingston I am a recent convert to Shakespeare's genius. He's just what the British public needs.

Larpent There's another one. This is most irregular.

Cautherley Three, sir!

Garrick It's quite simple – there are three brothers.

Larpent At the moment there is a worrying proliferation of kings. This last one seems a little outspoken.

Lady Kingston I am Lady Kingston.

Johnson It must be a form of insanity that has seized this unfortunate individual.

Lady Kingston I am the Countess of Bristol.

Johnson He is an insane melancholic.

Garrick I believe it is Lady Kingston.

Larpent He goes under many names, obviously.

Lady Kingston I came to this building to complain of a scurrilous show, which showed improper behaviour with a horsewhip.

Larpent *King Lear*?

Lady Kingston But the management have since given me complete satisfaction.

Larpent Nevertheless, serious accusations have been made. I'm afraid I cannot give this production my stamp of approval.

Johnson I assure you, sir. This fails to do justice to Shakespeare's greatest play. I advise you to read it at your leisure.

Goldsmith I read the original. Before lesser men saw fit to rewrite it.

Garrick You can't ban Shakespeare, the whole of the theatrical establishment would collapse.

Larpent The only way I could ever condone it would be to catalogue it as a musical. We tend to be more lenient with those.

Garrick *King Lear* definitely slots into that category.

Macklin Let's give him a number, Mr Garrick, and get it over with.

Garrick Very well. You begin, Mr Macklin.

Macklin After you, boss.

Hannah and Cautherley re-enter. The three Lears sing a song.

Garrick
'Blow winds and crack your cheeks.'

Macklin
I've been stuck in that basket it seems like weeks.

Lady Kingston
I don't know the words. What is it about?

Garrick
'You cataracts and hurricanoes spout.'

Macklin
I once was a king but they chucked me out.

All
Fa la la la. Fa la la.

Larpent That certainly clears matters up, thank you, Mr Garrick. Good day. (*He exits.*)

Cautherley I appear to be losing my grip on reality, Mr Garrick.

Hannah I no longer believe in the theatre as an organ of moral regeneration.

They exit.

Garrick Let us return to something approaching normality. Lady Kingston, a public apology will be read this evening.

Lady Kingston Thank you, Mr Garrick. I have complete faith in your abilities. (*She exits.*)

Johnson A most diverting morning, Davy. The pointless chatter of theatre folk always keeps my melancholy at bay.

Goldsmith There may be a moral here, Mr Garrick, but it'll take some thinking of.

Garrick I must apologise if you witnessed anything that may have offended your tastes, gentlemen.

Johnson It was harmless pleasure, Davy. To be able to furnish pleasure that is harmless, pure and unalloyed is as great a power as man can possess.

Lady Kingston (*offstage*) I appear to have mislaid my garters, Mr Garrick. You may find them in the basket.

Goldsmith May I remind you, sir, that my play was considered too low. (*He exits.*)

SCENE SIX

Garrick Success: the termination of any affair happy or unhappy. Success without any epitaph is commonly taken for good success.

THE AFTERPIECE: GARRICK'S OFFICE

Mrs Garrick All three Persian rugs are not Persian. They are in the style of Persia and were purchased in Bermondsey at thirty shillings for the original production of *Tancred and Sigismunda*.

Garrick Shite, in other words. (*Garrick operates his wig.*)

Mrs Garrick That's not coming with us.

Garrick That is a glorious piece of engineering.

Mrs Garrick writes in her ledger.

Mrs Garrick Tatty wig coming.

Garrick It's theatrical history, Mrs Garrick. Sheridan can have the building, but he's not having history.

Mrs Garrick I shouldn't think he'd want it. It's got fleas. What shall we do about the secret room?

Garrick Nothing at all.

Mrs Garrick It might be useful to Mr Sheridan.

Garrick Why would I wish to be useful to Mr Sheridan? He hasn't got the sort of wife who'd go in it.

Mrs Garrick Mr Sheridan has done us the favour of purchasing the patent, so we may retire with peace of mind.

Garrick He is our successor. We may wish him modest achievements. (*He picks a coat out of the skip, tries it on.*) Look at this, Mrs Garrick. (*He sports Goldsmith's jacket.*) He sold it to wardrobe. I always meant to get it back for him. (*He puts it on. He imitates Goldsmith.*) Now M–Mrs Garrick, who c–could I be?

Mrs Garrick They're making a fuss of him because of his play.

Garrick It'll die down. That's what fashion's like. It's fickle.

A knock at the door. She regards the secret door.

Mrs Garrick One last time.

She disappears into the secret room. Enter Dr Johnson. Garrick continues with his impersonation of Goldsmith.

Garrick G–good morning, Doctor.

Johnson So, you've heard.

Garrick Heard?

Johnson I'm presuming your bad taste is intentional. Our dear friend Goldsmith died this morning.

Garrick Died?

Johnson Four a.m. He accidentally poisoned himself with his own medicine. There's an irony in there somewhere, but I'm too upset to discover it.

Garrick He had an appointment to see me this afternoon.

Johnson He won't be coming.

Garrick I had good news for him. Mr Sheridan is anxious to commission him on my advice.

Johnson Dr Goldsmith, sir, has finished with earthly tasks. You had your chance to couple your name with his, sir, and you missed it. He has written the only play worth mentioning in fifty years.

Garrick That is an overstatement.

Johnson Only because you did not do it, Davy. Otherwise you would be agreeing with them heartily. His name is on everybody's lips. The town has declared him a genius.

Garrick A genius?

Johnson I do not condone what they are saying about you. Take my advice and ignore the whisperers.

Garrick The whisperers?

Johnson Those who accuse you of not joining your name to his. The greatest actor of the age with the greatest writer. I do not condone it because I allow nobody to attack you but myself.

Garrick These past weeks I have been most eager to assist Dr Goldsmith.

Johnson That is offering help to a drowning man after he has clambered exhausted to the shore. We are lonelier since he left us. I have others to see. Give my regards to Mrs Garrick. But I forget. She can hear me.

Garrick We'll meet soon.

Johnson That is not always in our hands, Davy.

He exits. Mrs Garrick enters. She points to Goldsmith's jacket.

Mrs Garrick Dr Johnson should have that. It's only right.

Garrick takes it off hurriedly. She goes to the door.

Garrick The whisperers!

She comes back.

Mrs Garrick It's Sam.

Garrick Sam!

Garrick composes himself. We hear off:

Cautherley Mrs Garrick.

Mrs Garrick It's good to see you again, Sam.

Cautherley enters.

Cautherley Mr Garrick.

Garrick Mr Cautherley.

Cautherley It's sad news.

Garrick Yes.

Cautherley I want to apologise, sir, for leaving the company so abruptly.

Garrick It is customary for actors to give a month's notice. I had to cast an Edmund, Banquo and Benvolio with very little grace.

Cautherley I'm sorry, sir.

Garrick But I'm glad you've come back, Sam. I've been wanting to talk to you.

Cautherley I don't want you to think I'm not grateful for the past, sir.

Garrick Did I ever tell you how I researched the part of Lear, Mr Cautherley?

Cautherley No, Mr Garrick.

Garrick I knew a man who killed his own child by accident. He was playing with her at a window when she slipped from his grasp and was dashed to death on the cobbles below. The poor man went mad with grief. He never left the room again but would sit in a chair staring at the window and every few minutes would rush to it with a cry as if reliving the dreadful moment over and over again. I used to visit him and it made me very sad, but there was also a part of me thinking: excellent, I can use that. The part of us that is an artist, Sam, can be quite hard, is what I'm trying to say. I know you have heard things while you've been here. Rumours.

Cautherley Rumours? I don't listen to them, sir.

Garrick I think you ought to know about your parents.

Cautherley I would not like to learn anything, sir, that compromised my respectability now I'm to be married.

Garrick Married!?

Cautherley To Miss More. We're going to start a school, sir.

Garrick To Miss More! Mr Cautherley. You are an actor, sir. You can't run a school.

Cautherley In Watford.

Garrick Don't give up, Mr Cautherley. Believe me, you have natural talent.

Hannah enters.

Hannah A school for poor and abandoned children, sir. A worthy cause.

Cautherley I shall be glad to be wanted. I shall shake your hand, sir. I doubt we'll have much time to visit.

Lady Kingston enters with everyone.

Lady Kingston Mr Garrick. Genius and national treasure.

Mrs Cibber Dear manager, dear, dear Garrick. How can we let this momentous day pass without acknowledging in some way your extraordinary achievements, your overwhelming talent.

Garrick This is a speech.

Mrs Cibber Please accept this token of our gratitude and esteem.

She hands Garrick the gloves. Garrick takes them, reads the card.

Garrick Shakespeare's gloves. Will you look at that, Mrs Garrick?

Mrs Garrick Lovely.

Mrs Cibber No one is aware of the sacrifices you've made. We might not have a theatre today, had you not ensured the respectability of our profession.

Applause.

Lady Kingston Mr Garrick, I hear you will be dining your way round the best homes in England performing a selection of after-dinner pieces. Perhaps you would oblige us?

All Yes. Oh yes, do, Mr Garrick, *etc.*

Garrick
'Howl, howl, howl! O you are men of stones!
Had I your tongues and eyes, I'd use them so
That heaven's vault should crack. She's gone for ever.
I know when one is dead and when one lives.
She's dead as earth.'

*A frisson runs through the crowd. He is performing
the prohibited version.*

'A plague upon you, murderers, traitors all!
I might have saved her, now she's gone for ever.'

Lady Kingston Mr Garrick. That is the wrong version.

Hannah We want the ending you rewrote so movingly.

Johnson The cruelty of the original cannot be countenanced by civilised people.

Mrs Garrick Give them what they want, Mr Garrick.

Garrick My apologies.

Mrs Cibber Perhaps I can oblige you. (*She arranges
herself as Cordelia.*)

Garrick
'I know when one is dead and when one lives.
The feather stirs! She lives. If it be so
It is a chance which will redeem all sorrows
That I have ever felt.'

Mrs Cibber   Oh happy time.

Garrick
          Is it possible?
Let the spheres stop their course, the sun make halt,
The winds be hush'd, the seas and fountains rest,
All Nature pause, and listen to the change.

Cordelia shall be a queen; winds catch the sound,
And bear it on your rosy wings to Heav'n –
Cordelia is a queen.
Our drooping country now erects her head,
Peace spreads her balmy wings and plenty blooming.
Divine Cordelia, all the Gods can witness
How much thy love to Empire I prefer!
Thy bright example shall continue the World
Whatever storms of Fortune are decreed
Truth and virtue shall at last succeed.

Mrs Garrick Bravo.

Lady Kingston Magnificent.

Garrick Thank you. Thank you. (*He loves the praise. He soaks it up. He bows.*) Thank you, thank you, thank you.

RESOURCE MATERIAL

by John Lennard

CONTEXT AND CONDITIONS

Elizabethan theatres are familiar from Shakespeare's Globe and many Victorian theatres survive in use, but Georgian theatres were different from either. They had a proscenium wall, but the stage extended well into what would now be the stalls and was divided: behind the proscenium wall was the 'scenic stage' or 'scene', a place of painted flats, careful tableaux, and the stylised, declamatory acting thought proper for tragedy; in front of the wall, flanked by stage-boxes and close to excitable patrons in the pit, was the 'forestage', a place of comedy where actors had to be quick with feet and tongue, ad-libs and audience-interactions. As Shakespeare used the 'above' and 'within' of the Globe, so later playwrights used the 'scenic' and 'forestages' (and the acting-styles that went with them) to drive and structure plays.

In such theatres playwrights and actors were at the mercy of audiences. The protocol of audience-silence developed only from the 1880s, when electricity made it possible to dim house-lights and the conventions of Ibsenite Naturalism outlawed address to the audience; Georgian house-lights stayed up throughout, and playgoers came and went, talked, cheered, or hissed at will, and thought themselves as much on show as the actors. Dr Johnson talked as loudly through tragedy as comedy, and was astonished one evening to be rebuked by Garrick for 'disturbing his feelings' as an actor. Though Garrick was a friend, Johnson was having none of it: "*Tush, sir, Mr Punch has no feelings*". And talk was the least of it: audiences came to praise or damn, and either way to make their feelings known. Favourite works, however hackneyed, were loudly demanded, and had better be supplied.

Performances were often interrupted, a new play or player deemed unpatriotic or disrespectful might be literally howled off stage, and audience-members who felt they or their friends (or England) had been insulted commonly demanded apologies from actors and/or managers before they would allow the show to continue. On one occasion Garrick was forced to apologise on his knees, and Drury Lane was substantially damaged by rioting at least six times during his managerial career – a mark of the casual rowdiness and resort to violence which was as characteristic of the eighteenth century as its elegance and intellectual devotion to reason.

Theatre-makers also faced more formal but equally stringent censors. Restoration theatre, fuelled by anti-Puritanism and female performers, was notably licentious, but after 1700 the pendulum began to swing, and the Licensing Act of 1737 transferred responsibility for plays from the ineffective Master of the Revels to the Lord Chamberlain. Only two London theatres, Covent Garden and Drury Lane, were licensed (others survived by performing musical drama) and scrutiny was tightened. By Victorian standards the eighteenth century remained dissolute, and theatre-goers continued to appreciate breeches parts (women showing their legs in male hose) and décolleté, yet Jacobethan and Restoration plays, including Shakespeare's, were considered unperformable as written, severely pruned of indelicacy, and generally 'improved'. The 'old comedy' of clowns and bawdy, cross-dressing heroines and low-life scenes, was eclipsed by 'weeping' or 'sentimental comedy', anaemically virtuous, piously predictable, but for decades the dominant vogue. Nor did tragedy escape: even *King Lear* was given a comedic ending in which Edgar marries Cordelia. Johnson thought "*Shakespeare has suffered the virtue of Cordelia to perish in a just cause, contrary to the natural ideas of justice, to the hope of the reader, and, what is yet more strange, to the faith of chronicles*", and heartily approved the success of Nahum Tate's rewrite:

In the present case the public has decided. Cordelia, from the time of Tate, has always retired with victory and felicity. And, if my sensations could add anything to the general suffrage, I might relate that I was many years ago so shocked by Cordelia's death that I know not whether I ever endured to read again the last scenes of the play till I undertook to revise them as an editor.

Garrick as Macbeth

DAVID GARRICK, ESQUIRE

Born in 1717, and raised (like Johnson) in Lichfield, Garrick dominated London theatre as actor-manager and writer from his debut in 1741 to his last performances in 1776. His theatre-works (including a score of plays and Shakespearean adaptations, plus satires, pantomimes, burlesques, and many prologues) fill seven volumes, and his long-term influence as a manager was enormous, but he made his name as an actor. Since the heyday of Thomas Betterton (c.1635-1710) and the great Restoration playwrights from Wycherley to Vanbrugh, theatre had declined in intensity and prestige, and acting become dully formulaic. Thomas Davies, Garrick's first biographer, says audiences *"had long been accustomed to an elevation of the voice, with a sudden mechanical depression of its tones, calculated to excite admiration, and to intrap applause. To the just modulation of the words, and concurring expression of the features from the genuine workings of nature, they had been strangers, at least for some time"* Garrick forcefully reintroduced a more naturalistic and sophisticated acting, first as a mesmeric Richard III, and within a year as Chamont in Otway's *Orphan*, his own *Lying Valet*, the Ghost in *Hamlet*, Bayes in Buckingham's *Rehearsal*, and a dozen others culminating (astonishingly for a 25-year old in his first season) in a King Lear its spectators never forgot. What riveted them was not Garrick's youth, but that this was the same actor who had played Richard and comedy. Writing to thank Garrick for his skills (and beg free tickets) Thomas Newton remarked *"The thing that strikes me above all others, is that variety in your acting, and your being so totally a different man in Lear from what you are in Richard. There is a sameness in every other actor [...] yours was an old man's passion, and an old man's voice and action; and in the four parts wherein I have seen you, Richard, Chamont, Bayes, and Lear, I never saw four actors more different from one another than you are from yourself."* Charles Macklin, the previous season's major hit with his tragic, vengeful Shylock, said the curse scene "seemed to electrify the audience [...] while [the] scene of the pathetic discovering his daughter Cordelia [...] drew tears of commiseration from the whole house". Garrick himself attributed success as Lear to having closely observed a man who accidentally killed his infant daughter and became deranged with guilty grief. Whatever his inspirations, ability to command audiences in tragedy and comedy with equal force and felicity made him a natural for Shakespeare, whose passionately mixed forms and brilliant indecorum Garrick explored throughout his career.

Garrick as Richard III

Yet for all his devotion to Shakespeare, culminating in the great Jubilee at Stratford in 1769, the original Shakespeare was exactly what the eighteenth century would not stomach, and Garrick's rôles, from Richard to Coriolanus and Benedick to Prospero, were lessened by the need to prune 'indelicacy'. Other notable triumphs, as Abel Drugger in Ben Jonson's *Alchemist* and Sir John Brute in Vanbrugh's *Provok'd Wife*, were similarly sanitised, and no part Garrick created, in his own plays or in weeping comedy, survives in the modern repertoire or deserves to. No great actor has been so ill-served by the temper of his age, and the difficulties he faced drove his theatrical innovations.

From 1747-76 Garrick was both star-attraction at Drury Lane and a co-licensee, in command of theatrical management. He controlled casting and repertoire, suiting himself to build a company willing to follow his lead, trawling Jacobethan and Restoration texts for plays that, even pruned, offered stronger meat and better rôles than new writing could supply. Audiences had to be placated to protect his income, reputation, and (for an actor) unprecedented social status, but over the years Garrick sought persistently to curtail and educate them. In the Prologue introducing his management, written by Johnson, Garrick assured auditors that *"The Stage but echoes back the publick Voice"* and *"The Drama's Laws the Drama's Patrons give, / For we that live to please, must please to live"*; reality proved more complex, and little by little Garrick created barriers between audience and actors that we now take for granted.

During the 1750s the Drury Lane public were successively excluded from the green room, other backstage areas, and the stage itself, the auditorium being enlarged to protect house-capacity and receipts. In the 1760s Garrick tried to end half-price admission after the third act, but was forced by rioting to give in; furious, he retired to France and Italy for two years, only to return with new lighting equipment which enabled the scenic stage to be enlarged and illuminated far more brightly and variably. This allowed more acting well away from the pit and stage-boxes, the beginning of a retreat behind the proscenium arch, and diminution of the forestage, which culminated in Ibsen's 'fourth wall' and the modern silencing of audiences. To capitalise on the new scenic stage Garrick imported designer Philippe de Loutherbourg (1740-1812), whose painting skills and technical ability to represent the natural light of various hours and seasons made Drury Lane the first great modern theatre of illusion. All this suited Garrick's naturalistic gifts, but curtailed liberties audiences had always taken for granted.

Garrick's health was indifferent (he suffered badly from gout), and in later years he managed more than he acted, but his reputation and social status never lessened. A friend of the great, frequently performing for royalty and a byword throughout Europe as the greatest actor of his time, his sudden death in 1779 was a sensation. Newspapers reported that 50,000 saw him lying in state, and his funeral procession had 33 six-horse coaches; he was buried in Westminster Abbey, below Kent's monument to Shakespeare. Johnson watched with a face 'bathed in tears', and bestowed on his friend his highest praise: *"he made his profession respectable"*.

GOLDSMITH'S *SHE STOOPS TO CONQUER*

Like many eighteenth-century writers, Goldsmith was Irish, from the clerical middle-classes impoverished by London's trade embargo and absentee landlords. He was also one of the oddest – a valued friend of Samuel Johnson, Joshua Reynolds, and Edmund Burke, but the licensed fool of their circle; the author of a major poem, an enduring novel, and a great play who never found a true métier; an habitual gambler and dandy, always in debt yet compulsively generous; a great talker prone to stuttering and a socialiser always uneasy with women.

Born at Lissoy in 1728, fifth in a large family, Goldsmith was sent (like his elder brother) to Trinity College, Dublin, to prepare for ordination. Poverty meant he went (in 1745) as a sizar, earning his way by waiting on fellow students, and in 1746 his father died, a financial and emotional blow which disrupted his studies; he did not graduate until 1750, and was never ordained. He tried law, then medicine, in Dublin, Edinburgh, Leiden and Padua, but gained no degree, and in 1756 settled in London to make his way in letters. Moderate successes with an *Enquiry into the Present State of Polite Learning in Europe* (1759) and the 'Chinese Letters' collected as *The Citizen of the World* (1762) could not save him endless hack-work, but brought contact with Johnson and in 1764 Goldsmith became, with Johnson, Burke, and Reynolds, a founder-member of the Turk's Head Club.

Despite poetic success with *The Traveller* (1764) and *The Deserted Village* (1770), and fictional success with *The Vicar of Wakefield* (1766), Goldsmith hankered for dramatic success but found himself at odds with Garrick (whom he had criticised in his *Enquiry*) and with the taste for weeping comedy. Honeywood, the hero of his first play, *The Good-Natur'd Man* (1766), is virtuous to the point of stupidity, borrowing to lend and too diffident to express himself; the plot turns on his need to become less virtuous, and Garrick, who read it, would not risk such satire of audience taste. George Colman was eventually persuaded to stage it at Covent Garden in 1768 (and promptly elected to the Turk's Head Club); it achieved a respectable nine performances, but the best scene, featuring some memorable bailiffs, was cut after the first, and the play was eclipsed by Garrick's rival production of Hugh Kelly's tear-stained *False Delicacy*, a howling success.

With *She Stoops to Conquer* (1771), Goldsmith abandoned the satirisation of sentimental comedy for richly laughing comedy in the old manner. The plot is from Bickerstaffe's *Love in a Village*; a far deeper debt to Shakespeare is evident in the disguised heroine, comedy of errors, low-life scenes, and dominating figure of Tony Lumpkin, vulgar and sensual, whose blunt self-interest and control of theatrical reality mark him as the finest comedic Vice since Feste. Johnson and most Club members understood what had been achieved, and Goldsmith formulated his case in an important Westminster Magazine essay comparing 'Laughing and Sentimental Comedy' (1773). Yet Colman sat on the play for a year, and in desperation Goldsmith offered it to Garrick, an opportunity at last for Garrick to premier a play, and create a rôle, that would endure in the repertoire; an opportunity he refused.

Garrick's thinking is moot. His provision of a prologue, admission to the Turk's Head Club, and failure to stage any rival production suggests tact, and tactics – the prologue is ambiguous, Garrick had long sought membership of the Club, and its members were loyal to Goldsmith. It may be that, with age, Garrick's theatrical antennae had weakened, that he did not foresee the waning of sentimental comedy that Goldsmith (and Sheridan) signalled; he may have guessed at it, but been happy to leave the new trend to his successors (he would retire in 1776). But *She Stoops to Conquer* is very much a forestage play, using the scenic stage only to create Hardcastle's house, and with vigorous action demanding the openness and engaged audience of the forestage – which makes it profoundly at odds with the innovative drive of Garrick's career, dedicated to greater naturalism and increased distance from a restrained audience.

The revival of laughing comedy was a powerful blow against the theatre of Garrick's dreams, which would not be achieved for another century; and Garrick probably knew it.

In the end the Club prevailed on Colman to stage *She Stoops* at Covent Garden in March 1773. Goldsmith was too nervous to attend, arriving only for Act 5. Colman's trepidation is indicated by his reaction to Goldsmith's alarm when Mrs Hardcastle's belief that her own garden is Crackskull Common was hissed: "*Psha! Doctor, don't be fearful of squibs, when we have been sitting almost these two hours upon a barrel of gunpowder*". But the rich comedy and career-making success of John Quick as Tony Lumpkin had done their work: laughter vanquished scandal and tears, and *She Stoops* has never since been out of the repertory for long.   Goldsmith signalled his triumph over Garrick in a mock-epitaph competition held by the Club that winter. Garrick extemporised a stinging couplet – '*Here lies Nolly Goldsmith, for shortness called Noll, / Who wrote like an angel but talked like poor Poll*.' – but Goldsmith produced a 'Retaliation' in which Garrick was acutely anatomised as "*a dupe to his art*":

Like an ill-judging beauty, his colours he spread,
And beplaster'd with rouge his own natural red.
On the stage he was natural, simple, affecting;
'Twas only that when he was off he was acting

With the essay on comedy and the success of *She Stoops*, Goldsmith's searing analysis of Garrick's faults capped his career and vindicated his tastes, but he did not live to enjoy his achievement. To the shock of Johnson and Burke (who wept at the news) and the lasting grief of Reynolds, Goldsmith died on Easter Monday 1774, of fever, and from self-administered purgatives. The scale of his debts led to a quiet burial in the Temple Church; a noble Latin epitaph by Johnson was later placed in Westminster Abbey. *The Deserted Village* and *The Vicar of Wakefield* were widely read well into the twentieth century, but it is for Tony Lumpkin that Noll has been longest remembered.

DE ANGELIS'S *A LAUGHING MATTER*

A co-commission by Out of Joint and the National Theatre, *A Laughing Matter* is April De Angelis's second play to dramatise theatre-history. In *Playhouse Creatures*, (Sphinx 1993, revived Old Vic 1997), her subject was the lives and status of Nell Gwynn and other women in Restoration theatre, vulnerable stars, trapped in celebrated unrespectablility and tyrannising authors whose every play must be a vehicle. As Mrs Betterton says to Thomas Otway when he protests at her demand for extensive cuts, "*Have you eaten lately, Mr Otway*". *A Laughing Matter* looks at the century that followed, celebrating the astonishing versatility of David Garrick and the vibrant company he managed, but posing against it the mysteries of Garrick's career and his late failure to recognise (or to act on) the brilliance of Goldsmith's *She Stoops to Conquer* (1771-73) – which Out of Joint staged in tandem.

Inevitably (and productively) *A Laughing Matter* compresses history a little, notably in making Spranger Barry somewhat younger and advancing Garrick's retirement; there is also an invented romance, between Samuel Cautherley and Hannah More, but in general, while particulars are imagined, both the history and its mysteries are very real. The Club founded by Samuel Johnson, Edmund Burke, Joshua Reynolds, and Oliver Goldsmith met in the Turk's Head in Gerrard Street every week from 1764; Garrick felt himself snubbed not to be invited to join, craved membership, and was finally admitted in 1773, probably to buy his support for *She Stoops*. Mrs Garrick, by birth an Austrian and in her youth a noted dancer, was by all accounts a judge whose opinions Garrick sought and trusted; she outlived him by 43 years, dying in 1822 at the age of 98 and still *"always talking of her dear Davey"* in a strongly Germanic accent. Samuel Cautherley was Garrick's dependent and protégé from at least the 1750s until a complete breach of relations in 1775, and persistently rumoured to be his illegitimate son, perhaps by the notorious Peg Woffington; nothing has ever been proven. And the Reverend Richard Cumberland, satirised by Sheridan as Sir Fretful Plagiary in *The Critic* (1779), certainly ground out a great number of sentimental plays, fairly written, perfectly actable, and great successes in their day. Most are fundamentally uninteresting (though *The Mysterious Husband* (1783) is a startling prose-tragedy and *The Jew* (1794) a notable indictment of anti-semitism) and with the exception of *The West Indian* (1771) now unperformed: but when Garrick had to choose between Cumberland and Goldsmith, *The West Indian* was a recent hit and Goldsmith an unproven maverick.

Equally real are the counterset scenes in the 1740s, when Garrick, in tense collusion with Charles Macklin, Woffington, and others, began to manoeuvre for managerial control. Though Garrick's revolution brought financial security to the theatre and improved pay and conditions to actors, his commitment to greater naturalism and contempt for prating oration threatened established stars, as his demands for professionalism, sobriety, and rehearsal challenged established egos. Even an actor of Garrick's wild talent could not have ruled Drury Lane for thirty years without a wide streak of ruthlessness and (until Goldsmith) an almost infallible nose for maximal profit: but the new writing he staged has long been discarded from the repertoire, and the eighteenth-century plays that are remembered are from the age of Farquhar and Congreve, before Garrick's coming, and the age of Sheridan, after his passing. A great deal is known about Garrick: few actors have been more analysed or as biographised, but he remains a mass of contradictions, an actor so consummate that he escapes academic wranglings and is best considered through his own preferred medium and habitat: as another playhouse creature.

THE PLAYERS

The Turk's Head Club

DR SAMUEL JOHNSON (1709-84) was the great intellectual heavyweight of his century: an essayist, poet, lexicographer, and critic of the first rank, a translator and novelist of quality, the subject of Boswell's magisterial *Life*, and a failed dramatist. Garrick staged his tragedy *Irene* in 1749 and single-handedly kept it going for nine nights, but it was

SAMUEL JOHNSON

never revived and though Johnson and Garrick were childhood friends there is often a sharpness to Johnson's remarks about Garrick and theatre. The *Preface to Shakespeare* (1765), however, was the most important critical essay for nearly a century, and *Lives of the Poets* (1779-81) treats many dramatists with sensitive intelligence. A founder-member of the Club in 1764.

OLIVER GOLDSMITH (1728-74) of impoverished Irish clerical stock, was a bundle of contradictions – a social clown whose elegiac satire, *The Deserted Village*, was rated by Johnson as the best couplet-poem since Pope, and whose nostalgic revival in *She Stoops to Conquer* of the old 'laughing comedy' signalled the beginning of the end for 'weeping comedy'. A founder-member of the Club in 1764.

OLIVER GOLDSMITH

SIR JOSHUA REYNOLDS (1723-92) was England's greatest portrait-painter, ranked by Ruskin as one of the seven greatest colourists. He rose to prominence in the early 1750s, and in 1759 had 156 sitters and earned £6,000; elected in 1768 as the first president of the Royal Academy, he was knighted in 1769. A close friend of Goldsmith's, his memoir offers the most sympathetic and thoughtful contemporary account. The principal founder-member of the Club in 1764, he conceived it to give Johnson 'unlimited opportunities for talking'.

SIR JOSHUA REYNOLDS

EDMUND BURKE (1729-97) was an Irish lawyer, statesman, political philosopher, essayist, and MP, who became steadily more prominent from the mid-1760s and was widely thought the finest orator of his day. A founder-member of the Club in 1764.

EDMUND BURKE

JAMES BOSWELL (1740-95) still thought by many the greatest of biographers, was a Scots lawyer with insatiable appetites for company and women who spent as much time as possible in London. He met Johnson in 1763, and fast became his intimate, touring Scotland and the Hebrides with him in 1773 and assembling the materials from which he built his *Life of Johnson*, dedicated to Reynolds and published in 1791. Throughout the nineteenth century Boswell was worshipped as a biographer, but the discovery of two great caches of private papers have revealed his range, complexity, and contradictions Elected to the Club in 1773.

JAMES BOSWELL

Garrick & Co.

DAVID GARRICK (1717-79) the greatest actor of his age, was also a prolific dramatist, and manager of Drury Lane 1747-76. He acquired an unprecedented social standing for an actor, and did much to help establish Shakespeare as the national bard, organising the first great celebration of him, a Jubilee at Stratford in 1769. Elected to the Turk's Head Club in 1773.

EVA VEIGEL GARRICK (1724-1822) born in Vienna, made her professional London debut in 1746 as the dancer 'Violette', and was a sensation for three years, both on stage and in becoming a protegé of Lady Burlington and a court-favourite. After marrying Garrick in 1749 she abandoned performance but retained her aristocratic connections and worked closely with him, socially and behind the scenes, throughout his career.

SAMUEL CAUTHERLEY (*c*. 1745-1805) made his debut as a child-actor in 1755, and was rumoured to be Garrick's illegitimate son by Peg Woffington or Jane Hippisley. The truth is lost, but the Garricks (who were childless) certainly raised Cautherley and paid for his education. He made his adult debut in 1766, but lacked talent or was unable to turn his hand to parts he found uncongenial. He withdrew from the stage a few weeks into the 1775 season, causing a complete breach with the Garricks.

HANNAH MORE (1745-1833) a deeply religious woman attracted to the pieties of 'weeping comedy', met David and Eva Garrick in the early 1770s and became a family intimate. He secured a production of her tragedy *Percy* in 1777, and of *Fatal Falsehood* in 1779, but after his death she came to think playgoing wrong and turned to writing pious pamphlets. The founder of the Religious Tract Society (1799), she left more than £30,000 to religious charities.

HANNAH MORE

The Drury Lane Actors

MRS (ANN) BARRY (1734-1801) née Street, formerly Dancer, made her debut in the 1750s and became Spranger Barry's partner, then wife, in the 1760s. She found major success as his female leads both in Shakespeare and 'weeping comedy', and after his death continued to appear until 1798.

SPRANGER BARRY (1717-77) an Irish actor-manager, was perhaps Garrick's major rival (at Covent Garden) and collaborator (at Drury Lane) – rôles between which he oscillated throughout his career. There was a famous clash of Romeos in 1750, and a pointed Lear in 1756. After a financially distastrous interlude in Dublin and Cork, he returned to London in 1767, frequently acting for and with Garrick in the 1760s-70s, and almost as frequently quarrelling. (He is somewhat fictionalised in *A Laughing Matter*).

MRS (SUSANNA) CIBBER (1714-66) sister of the composer Thomas Arne, was a leading tragedienne of the 1730s, famed for pathos and weeping. She was forced to leave the stage in 1739 when her husband Theophilus, having encouraged her to have an affair with a man called Sloper to whom he owed money, sued Sloper for adultery, demanding £5000 in damages. (He was awarded a desultory £10 by a scandalised jury, and until his death by drowning in 1758 was frequently hissed from the stage). She returned in 1742 to sing the contralto arias in the first performance of Handel's *Messiah*, and once again became a firm favourite, continuing despite recurrent illnesses to act and sing until her death.

RICHARD CROSS (d. 1760) a versatile actor and dancer, served from 1741 as the prompter at Drury Lane, a job that required him to fill in for anyone failing to turn up. His diaries, laconic and shrewd, are a significant source for theatre-historians.

CHARLES MACKLIN (1699-1797) was an Irish actor, manager, and playwright who found London fame in the 1730s, as Peachum in *The Beggar's Opera* in 1736, with a conviction for manslaughter in 1739 following a quarrel over a stage-wig, and as a fiercely vengeful Shylock in 1740 – a performance Pope praised as "*the Jew / That Shakespeare drew*". A forerunner of Garrick's in reintroducing a more naturalistic style, Macklin helped train Garrick to play Lear, but for unknown reasons probably to do with clashing egos was

CHARLES MACKLIN

excluded from the settlement of the actors' dispute in 1743 and thereafter held a grudge against Garrick; he did, however, open Garrick's first managerial season as Shylock. Notable also for a heavily Scottish *Macbeth* in 1774, he retired only in 1789 when his memory began to fail.

MRS (PEG) WOFFINGTON (1714-60) a fiery Irish actor, found adult fame in the breeches part of Sir Harry Wildair in Farquhar's *Constant Couple* in 1740. Lady Anne to Garrick's Richard III in 1741, and Cordelia to his Lear in the same season, she became his mistress but apparently refused to marry him, and left Drury Lane in 1748. Notorious for her varied amours, and for once stabbing her rival Mrs Bellamy, she collapsed on stage in 1757 while delivering the epilogue to *As You Like It* and never recovered.

PEG WOFFINGTON

And Others

GEORGE COLMAN the Elder (1732-94) was an Oxford-educated lawyer whom friendship with Garrick turned to dramatic authorship in 1760. He translated Terence and Horace, and edited Beaumont & Fletcher, but is remembered as manager of Covent Garden 1767-74, and of the Haymarket Theatre 1777-89 (in which he was succeeded by his son). Elected to the Club in 1768, probably as a *quid pro quo* for his agreement to stage Goldsmith's *The Good-Natur'd Man*.

REVD RICHARD CUMBERLAND (1732-1811) came to authorship relatively late. A sometime fellow of Trinity College, Cambridge, he became private secretary to Lord Halifax, a government minister, in 1761, and by the mid-1770s was secretary to the Board of Trade (he even negotiated a Spanish Treaty in 1780). But as a young man he had seen Garrick act, and from the later 1760s became a dependable author of 'weeping comedies' that did good business then but are now forgotten (with the occasional exception of *The West Indian*) Though famously lampooned as 'Sir Fretful Plagiary' by Sheridan in *The Critic*, he continued to write and to be performed into the 1800s.

LADY KINGSTON (1720-88) née Elizabeth Chudleigh, was an astonishing woman described in the *Dictionary of National Biography* as "beautiful, but weak-minded, and illiterate", her racy life included a secret marriage to an Earl's brother, open concubinage, flirtations with George II, a public marriage to a Duke, a conviction in the House of Lords for bigamy, and a late friendship with Catherine the Great of Russia. Along the way she found time briefly to patronise the Revd Cumberland.

CHARLES FLEETWOOD (d. *c*.1745) was a wealthy theatregoer who in 1733 purchased the Drury Lane Patent and became manager, first in partnership with Colley Cibber, then with Macklin. He introduced some necessary though unpopular reforms, notably ending the free admission of servants to the Footman's Gallery, and in 1742 secured the services of Garrick for the theatre, but was financially irresponsible and brought Drury Lane to the brink of bankruptcy before selling his share of the patent to James Lacy (later Garrick's managerial partner) in 1744.

THE LORD CHAMBERLAIN, nominally a court official appointed by the monarch but in practice a government post, was from 1737 responsible both for licensing all theatre-buildings except the Patent Theatres, and for vetting all new or rewritten scripts for performance. The bulk of the work was done by a small team of Examiners of Plays. Severity of control varied from incumbent to incumbent and with the political wind, especially where 'indecency' was concerned, but the censorship of anything considered blasphemous or political was always stringent; even in the 1950s and 1960s works by Beckett and Osborne were censored for blasphemy. The system was abolished only in 1968. During the dispute about *She Stoops to Conquer* in 1773 the Lord Chamberlain was Francis Seymour, Marquess of Hertford, and the chief Examiner of Plays was William Chetwynd, assisted by the Shakespearean scholar and editor Edward Capell.

FROM BOSWELL'S *LIFE OF JOHNSON* (1791)
[*James Boswell, The Life of Samuel Johnson, LL.D.* [ed. R. W. Chapman, 1904; 3rd ed. rev. Oxford: Oxford University Press, 1980 (World's Classics)])

February 1749. "On occasion of his play being brought upon the stage, Johnson had a fancy that as a dramatick author his dress should be more gay than what he ordinarily wore; he therefore appeared behind the scenes, and even in one of the side boxes, in a scarlet waistcoat, with rich gold lace, and a gold-laced hat. He humourously observed to Mr.

Langton, 'that when in that dress he could not treat people with the same ease as when in his usual plain clothes ' Dress indeed, we must allow, has more effect even upon strong minds than one should suppose, without having had the experience of it. His necessary attendance while his play was in rehearsal, and during its performance, brought him acquainted with many of the performers of both sexes, which produced a more favourable opinion of their profession than he had harshly expressed in his *Life of Savage*. With some of them he kept up an acquaintance as long as he and they lived, and was ever ready to shew them acts of kindness. He for a considerable time used to frequent the Green Room, and seemed to take delight in dissipating his gloom, by mixing in the sprightly chit-chat of the motley circle then to be found there. Mr. David Hume related to me from Mr. Garrick, that Johnson at last denied himself this amusement, from considerations of rigid virtue; saying 'I'll come no more behind your scenes, David; for the silk stockings and white bosoms of your actresses excite my amorous propensities '

Saturday 25 June, 1763 "[Goldsmith's] mind resembled a fertile, but thin soil. There was a quick, but not a strong vegetation, of whatever chanced to be thrown upon it. No deep root could be struck. The oak of the forest did not grow there; but the elegant shrubbery and the fragrant parterre appeared in gay succession. It has been generally circulated and believed that he was a mere fool in conversation; but, in truth, this has been greatly exaggerated. He had, no doubt, a more than common share of that hurry of ideas which we often find in his countrymen, and which sometimes produces a laughable confusion in expressing them. He was very much what the French call *un étourdi*, and from vanity and an eager desire of being conspicuous wherever he was, he frequently talked carelessly without knowledge of the subject, or even without thought. His person was short, his countenance coarse and vulgar, his deportment that of a scholar aukwardly affecting the easy gentleman."

FROM JOHN GINGER'S *THE NOTABLE MAN, THE LIFE AND TIMES OF OLIVER GOLDSMITH* (London, Hamish Hamilton, 1977)

During this decade when his writings were winning for him the reputation of an always rational observer of the social scene, of a man whose lucid style combined common sense with intuition and humour with feeling, it must have been deeply refreshing for Goldsmith to relapse into the temporary anonymity of a playgoer and, through this short but vital dramatic rôle, to enjoy vicariously the pleasures of a thoroughly disreputable existence. The need to put [Lumpkin] at the centre of his own play, even at the risk of producing an anomalous and déclassé character, suggests that there had been an imaginative spilling-over from an area of his personality where the identification with a Vice/satyr figure was not only possible but psychologically necessary. The difference between appearance and reality was a theme which for a long time had hovered uncertainly on the borders of the terrain over which he had imaginative control. There had been an attempt to take it up in [*The Good-Natur'd Man*] but, after hints that Honeywood's seeming altruism sprang from a less worthy impulse, he had failed to develop the theme. By the time of his withdrawal to Hyde in the summer after the publication of *The Deserted Village* there was a much more pressing need to come to grips with it, and this need would give [*She Stoops to Conquer*] its dynamic. Whether it is Marlow veering from insolent self-assurance to stammering inadequacy, or the heir to £1,500 a year with the manners and tastes of a peasant, or the mother who clings stubbornly and against all the evidence to the belief that her ugly duckling is about to turn into a swan, the consequences of illusion are to be encountered at every turn.

GLOSSARY

above In Jacobethan amphitheatres (such as the Globe) the first floor and balcony of the tiring-house, used for Juliet's balcony, castle battlements etc.

ad lib from Latin *ad libitum*, 'with freedom, at will'. An improvised line, not pre-written and learned but made up by an actor in peformance, or the action of speaking such lines. In modern theatre, ad libbing may be used as a rehearsal technique but is rare in mainstream performances of fully scripted plays.

bawdy from bawd, a female procurer or pandar. Humorous indecency in language and gesture; low jokes and double entendres, esp. in Shakespeare and other Jacobethan playwrights.

benefit An eighteenth-century system for giving additional payment to authors and actors. Authors were entitled to the profits of the ninth performance of their plays (hence the urgent need to play for at least nine nights), and if a show was a big hit further benefit nights might be granted; payments could amount to several hundred pounds, the equivalent of many thousands today. The leading actors of the company also usually received one benefit night in each season, for which they could choose the plays to be performed. Though a voluntary system, benefits continued to be given throughout the eighteenth century, but were eroded in the nineteenth and (after a series of dramatic copyright acts) slowly replaced by other forms of profit-sharing, often less generous. (Cf. modern benefit games or seasons in professional sports.)

breeches part A male rôle (written to be) played by a female actor, who would display her legs by wearing breeches (short, close-fitting trousers). Popular in the eighteenth century, but largely disapproved of in the nineteenth, the tradition survives in the Principal Boy in pantomime.

burlesque from Italian *burla*, 'a joke'. A work which parodies another work, or pastiches a particular style; both noun and verb.

comedic Concerning the structure and/or nature of comedy; a usefully narrower term than 'comic'. Thus to end with a wedding is certainly comedic, but may not be 'comic'. ('Tragic' and 'tragedic' may be similarly distinguished)

comedy from Greek κωμος [komos], a revel. One of the two fundamental Greek dramatic genres, paired with tragedy. Neo-classical theorists insisted that certain things were essential to comedy (e.g. that it must deal with society, not individuals; that it must end in marriage; that there must be no deaths etc.), and similar views remain common. The distinction of the dramatic genres, however, is dependent on theatre-practice: in ancient Greece comedy and tragedy were performed by different actors wearing different kinds of masks and costumes at different times of the year during distinct festivals, and were as clearly separate as art and sport are to us; in modern theatre, where the same company perform both genres at the same venue, comedy and tragedy form a continuum, and many plays draw equally on both. It remains true, of course, that tragedic elements of a play will tend to be sad or violent, and comedic ones funny, celebratory, or peaceful, but almost every dramatist of interest challenges the distinction as much as endorsing it. Because the term 'comedy' is so broad many variants have been labelled, including Greek Old, Middle, and New Comedy; Roman Plautine Comedy (by Plautus); Italian *Commedia dell'arte* and *Commedia erudita*; Renaissance Citizen or City Comedy, Shakespeare's dark comedy, and Jonson's Comedy of Humours; Restoration Comedy; eighteenth-century weeping or sentimental comedy; low comedy; nineteenth-century musical comedy and comic opera; and modern black comedy, screwball comedy, stand-up comedy, teen comedy and situation comedy or sitcom.

decorum from Latin *decorus*, 'graceful, adorned'. The general meaning is 'seemliness, appropriate behaviour', but in neo-classical dramatic and genre theory 'generic decorum' is the idea that genres should be 'pure' i.e. that comedies should avoid death, tragedies avoid laughter etc , and that in performance the acting style, costume, dialogue etc. should conform with generic expectations. This applies as much to cinematic and televisual genres as to the stage: thus in a Western there should be white cowboys who drink, swear, and fight, Indians on horseback, stagecoaches etc , while in Science Fiction there should be aliens, spaceships etc ; a highly-educated cowboy, or a horse in an SF movie, are equally indecorous.

editor (1) In academia, a person who prepares for publication the work of another writer. (2) In publishing, the author's main contact at the publisher, who oversees the process of publication.

epilogue A speech at the end of a play, usually delivered directly to the audience. It may be spoken by a choric figure or by one of the rôles, but in Restoration and eighteenth-century theatre is often spoken by a leading actor in their own person.

flats Wooden frames covered with cloth on which perspectival scenes are painted. They cannot be properly used in any theatre lacking a proscenium arch (which focuses the audience's sight-lines), and so were unknown in Jacobethan public theatres, and are not used in modern studio-theatres or black holes; in eighteenth-century theatres they were used intensively, but of necessity restricted to the scenic stage.

forestage In Restoration and eighteenth-century theatres that part of the stage in front of the proscenium wall, surrounded by the stage-boxes and fronting directly onto the pit.

fourth wall In full-blown Ibsenite Naturalism, as performed in proscenium-arch theatres, an imaginary one-way mirror filling the proscenium arch. The implication is that actors should act wholly in their characters, not even knowing an audience are there. The term cannot sensibly be applied to any theatre without a proscenium wall and arch.

house-lights The lights in the auditorium. Dimming of house-lights during performance was not possible before the introduction of electricity, and the modern protocol of spectating-in-darkness dates only from the late nineteenth-century. The dimming of house-lights was the most important factor in making audiences keep silent during performance; modern audiences at the National Theatre and at Shakespeare's Globe behave quite differently.

Ibsenite Naturalism 'Ibsenite' is the adjective from Norwegian playwright Henrik Ibsen (1828-1906), the spear- and figure-head of a dramatic revolution in the 1880s and '90s; 'Naturalism' (with a capital N) is a theory of production and performance which calls for as naturalistic an acting-style as possible + realist (as opposed to painted or illusory) sets. 'Ibsenite Naturalism', as embodied in Ibsen's mature plays, is the strictest form, disallowing any breach of the 'fourth wall', all soliloquy (unless very short and naturalised as a character talking to him/herself), all metatheatrical reference etc . Full-blown Ibsenite Naturalism is particularly associated with the use of box-sets in proscenium-arch theatres, and is now uncommon on stage, but was a major influence on the great Russian actor-trainer Constantin Stanislavski (1865-1938); transmitted (with severe distortions) via the 'Method' taught by American Lee Strasberg (1901-82) at the Actors' Studio in New York, it remains a powerful norm in film and TV.

Jacobethan Strictly, of the period 1558-1625; more commonly, the period of the Shakespearean theatre, 1576-1642. A portmanteau word formed from 'Elizabethan' and 'Jacobean', it is useful because the careers of Shakespeare and many of his fellows straddle the reigns of Elizabeth I (1558-1603) and James VI & I (1603-1625).

low A cant word in the eighteenth century for anything considered coarse, vulgar, or otherwise improper; it survives in a 'low blow' (from boxing, a punch below the belt intended to strike the testicles), and in 'low church'. Low comedy was typically bawdy, but might also be closer to farce and/or slapstick than weeping comedy allowed; low comedians tended to perform physically rather than cleverly or verbally, and often relied on stock jokes, props, and costumes as well as traditional double entendres. The *Carry On* films are an obvious modern instance of low comedy, Benny Hill of a low comedian.

Mr Punch The nutcracker-faced puppet protagonist of Punch-and-Judy Shows, a wife-beater often in trouble with a policeman because his dog Toby is a sausage-thief. Emerging in the mid-seventeenth century, Mr Punch is derived from the figure of Pulcinella (= 'little chicken'), usually a bossy and interfering shop-keeper, in Italian *Commedia dell'arte*.

naturalistic A complex word made very difficult by careless, variable, and ill-defined critical use. Often confused with 'realist' (a term applying primarily to set-design), and with 'Ibsenite Naturalism', 'naturalistic' is most usefully defined as referring to the minimisation of the gap between an actor and the rôle that actor plays. It may therefore be thought of as the opposite of 'stylised', but it is crucial to remember that each element of a performance (physical style, delivery, costume, props) may be more or less naturalistic or stylised. At one extreme TV and film usually seem highly naturalistic, but may contain very stylised elements (vapid dialogue, impossible fights, car chases etc), while at the other musicals, opera, ballet, and many non-European theatre-forms are fundamentally non-naturalistic. In e.g. the Monty Python 'Ministry of Silly Walks' John Cleese's costume and delivery are overtly naturalistic, but the movement is ludicrously stylised, and the humour arises not just from the absurd style but from the clash of naturalistic and non-naturalistic elements. Contrary to much casual belief, Shakespeare is not generally naturalistic, and his plays do not respond well to rigidly naturalistic acting.

pantomime The only indigenous English theatre-form, invented by John Rich (1682-1781), who in the early eighteenth century began adapting elements of *Commedia dell'arte* (esp. the figure of Arlecchino, or 'Harlequin') for London stage-performance. The form rapidly became very popular, and in the nineteenth century developed the fairy-tale plots, routines of audience-participation, and stock-rôles that survive to the present, including the Pantomime Dame (played by a man), Principal Boy (played by a woman), Pantomime Horse or Cow (played by two actors, one having to be the rear end), and Benevolent Agent (e.g. the Fairy Godmother). Modern English pantomime, performed around Christmas and a financial mainstay for many theatres, is notable for its use of TV stars and substantial annual rewriting to incorporate topical jokes.

Patent Theatres In 1661 two London companies were granted licences (or Patents) to act in the capital, but both companies moved between theatres. After the licensing Act of 1737, the licences became tied to the Theatres Royal in Covent Garden and Drury Lane, which became known as the Patent Theatres. The official duopoly enjoyed by the Patent Theatres was abolished in 1843, but the Patents themselves continue to exist as integral parts of the charters of the two theatres.

pit In Jacobethan, Restoration, and eighteenth-century theatres the audience-area immediately in front (and to the sides) of the (fore)stage, where the modern stalls would be; associated at first with the poorest, least educated playgoers, it later became the favoured place of rowdier playgoers of many classes, and remained partly a standing-area well into the eighteenth century.

prologue A speech at the beginning of a play, usually delivered directly to the audience. It may be spoken by a choric figure or by one of the rôles, but in Restoration and eighteenth-century theatre is often spoken by a leading actor in their own person.

proscenium arch The arched or square opening in the proscenium wall through which the audience (on one side) watch the actors (on the other); a framing device for audiences necessary to the use of flats bearing painted scenes in perspective.

proscenium wall A wall dividing some theatres into an area for the audience and the stage + backstage area; it is pierced by the proscenium arch.

Restoration The return of Charles II in 1660, restoring the monarchy lost when his father, Charles I, was executed in 1649; Restoration drama is the period from the 1661 re-opening of the theatres (closed in 1642) until the early eighteenth century. Major playwrights include John Dryden (1631-1700), George Etherege (1636-92), William Wycherley (1641-1715), Thomas Otway (1652-85), John Vanbrugh (1664-1726), and William Congreve (1670-1729); leading actors include Thomas Betterton (*c.* 1635-1710), Nell Gwynn (*c.* 1650-87), Elizabeth Barry (*c.* 1658-1713), and Anne Bracegirdle (1671-1748). Restoration Comedy was notable for the advent of female actors, is generally fairly bawdy, was by all accounts a hoot in performance, and remains in the reperoire; Restoration Tragedy tends to be highly stylised and is now often found overwrought, so it is rarely performed.

satire from late Latin *satira*, 'a medley'; cf. satyr. Originally a composite genre, featuring a variety of forms, modes etc., but subsequently dominated by one kind of form prevalent in satires, the attack on contemporary figures and ideas to expose folly and vice. Satire of this kind was originally a part of Greek Old Comedy, and modern satire remains close to comedy (including stand-up) but difficult to accommodate in tragedy or epic without damaging their gravity.

scenic stage or **scene** In Restoration and eighteenth-century theatres that part of the stage behind the proscenium wall, where painted flats and backdrops were used to create perspectival illusion. The term 'scene' is often used in playtexts of the period to indicate a change of flats or the movement of actors between the scenic and forestages.

sentimental comedy see weeping comedy

Shakespeare's Globe The close replica of the original Globe Theatre on the south bank of the Thames in London, near the site of the original Globe; it opened in 1997, and is also known as Globe III. Globe I was the first theatre, moved to the south-bank site in 1599, and was the building for which Shakespeare wrote most of his mature work; it burned down in 1613. Globe II was its replacement, built in 1613, closed in 1642, and demolished in 1644.

tableau(x) from Old French *tablel*, 'a little table'. A stage-equivalent of the 'freeze-frame', a moment in which actors are posed in a significant arrangement, forming a picture. Though common in non-naturalistic forms, tableaux are esp. associated with nineteenth-century plays and melodrama, particularly as a final stage-direction; the ending of Ibsen's *Hedda Gabler* both uses and parodies such a tableau.

weeping comedy A popular, rather scornful name for 'sentimental comedy', a form dominating the mid-eighteenth century from the severe Licensing Act of 1737 to the 1770s, and surviving well into the nineteenth century. It is characterised by the exhibition of Christian piety, hypersensitive sexual propriety, unimpeachable (and effectively untested) morals, and vapid predictability; bawdy dialogue and low-life scenes (e.g. in taverns) were utterly excluded, as were most things anyone today would find funny.

within In Jacobethan amphitheatres (such as the Globe) the inside of the tiring-house, where actors heard but not seen by the audience could play people on the other side of a door, wall etc ; the stage-direction 'within' occurs 73 times in Shakespeare's First Folio, and in most instances would most obviously be staged by using the central, curtained exit/entrance known as the 'discovery-space'.

A full glossary of theatrical and critical terms can be found in John Lennard & Mary Luckhurst, *The Drama Handbook: A guide to reading plays* (Oxford University Press paperback, 2002; ISBN 0-19-870070-9; £12.99)

All illustrations by Marco Nesbit, except where marked.